The Laughing Wagner
his Wit, Puns, Pranks & Dare-Devil Stunts

Joachim Köhler

Translated from the German by
Tom Artin

Copyright © 2015 Joachim Köhler
All rights reserved.

FreeScholarPress™

Original title: *Der lachende Wagner. Das unbekannte Leben des Bayreuther Meisters Richard Wagner*
by Joachim Köhler
© 2012 by Wilhelm Heyne Verlag, München
a division of Verlagsgruppe Random House GmbH,
München, Germany.

ISBN-13: 978-0692528532
ISBN-10: 0692528539

For my Parents

Contents

Prologue   1

Act One: A Kind of Mad Genius
- Scene 1. "A Cherub from Olympic Regions"   13
- Scene 2. A Man Stands on his Head   25
- Scene 3. The Nose of God   32
- Scene 4. The Return of Kapellmeister Kreisler   39

Act Two: A Dog's Life
- Scene 1. The Tympani Fiasco   53
- Scene 2. In the Realm of the Fairy Amorosa   72
- Scene 3. Between Peps and Papo   78
- Scene 4. Fantasy Pieces In Callot's Manner   93

Act Three: The "Seven Wonders of the World"
- Scene 1. Sorrows of the Young Tin-pot Potentate   113
- Scene 2. When Tannhäuser Wed Elisabeth   125
- Scene 3. Water Music for 50 Spiked Helmets   142
- Scene 4. Liebestod and Schadenfreude   154
- Scene 5. "My Niebelung Operettas"   172
- Scene 6. In the Mystical Red-Light District   191

Act Four: "Harlequin Must Die!"
- Scene 1. "Tomorrow, We Let the Devil Loose!"   203
- Scene 2. Züs Bünzli's Sister   211
- Scene 3. The Praying Mantis   229
- Scene 4. "From Heaven Through the World to Hell"   237

Epilogue: 249

Index of Names   253

Prologue

This book ventures into uncharted territory. Wagner's humor is considered dubious; scholarship avoids it like a minefield. On principle alone, the Bayreuth Master is not regarded as funny; even less are those who find him funny. No laughing Wagner makes his appearance in the canon of his admirers, let alone in the attacks of his detractors.

One hesitates to see him as light-hearted, not least lest humor relativistically leaven the moral verdict that in his case is already severe enough. Nothing can negate Wagner's anti-Semitism—who can doubt it?—surely not his laughter, which would be unseemly in any case. On the other hand, not even Wagner's inexcusable weaknesses can negate his laughter.

Whoever would take Wagner seriously, for good or ill, must also take his humor seriously, endure his laughter. In the process, he may well catch himself laughing involuntarily along with him. The picture of him one has gathered . . . might just unexpectedly slip away. One scarcely trusts one's eyes and ears: is he truly like that?

The Wagner who steps onto the comedy stage here has doffed that classical mask, familiar to the point of cliché. His expression lightens, his face is transformed into a mocking smile. It is worth listening when this great ironist, freed from his established role, begins speaking freely, sparing neither his public nor himself from his wit. A great unknown cynic, philosophically as well as temperamentally, is presented here, or rather, laughing, will present himself.

This book seeks not to judge but to report. One might consider it an essay in "gay science," as Friedrich Nietzsche sketched it. Wagner's most illustrious apprentice sought thereby to create a counter-model to the Bayreuth ideology, whose deadly seriousness he found ludicrous. At the same time the composer and Master of the Festival Theater himself offered up the counter-model to Bayreuth's deadly solemnity. Wagner was himself the anti-Wagner Nietzsche aspired to be. The philosopher could have learned the laughter with which he sought to counter the Bayreuth cult from the Master whom he loved and hated.

From the perspective of such a "gay science," Wagner—the putative insufferable ego-maniac—turns out to be an irresistible perennial communicator, who remains creative even in his foibles, and retains his self-irony even in anger. "In the midst of bitterness," he commented, "sparkles wit!"[1]

He always derived pleasure from the self-irony he played off his interlocutors as much as himself. His wife, Cosima, guardian of the Bayreuth grail, could never reconcile herself to his "rapid shifts from seriousness to humor,"[2] which bewildered his disciples too: was what the Master himself just uttered to be taken seriously, or was he amusing himself at another's expense? Did he lapse into ecstasy or was he only

---

[1] *Cosima Wagner's Diaries*, July 8, 1979.
[2] *ibid.*, March 8, 1882.

The Laughing Wagner

playing the fool? After playing Isolde's *Liebestod*, why did he crawl under the Bechstein and howl like a dog?

Although Cosima considered herself the greatest Wagner expert, she had no answer to his lightning character reversals by which he occasionally transformed the pilgrimage site of Bayreuth into a coarse comic stage. This "so characteristic, unmediated transition from seriousness to humor" was immediately legible on his face: "Like lightning, humor appears where heavy clouds of melancholy had weighed upon his eyes."[3]

The attempts of his devoted disciples to understand him, as well as his wife's efforts at civilizing him both foundered on his predilection for joking at everyone's expense, including his own. Wagner never allowed himself to be buttoned up by Cosima's stiff grandeur and its eternal reproduction by the Wagnerites, in whose company laughter is stilled forever. Instead, he took the liberty of mocking the exalted picture they had constructed of him. Wagner projected the perfect embodiment of the "gay science," even before Nietzsche had devised it against him.

This enigmatic figure behind his shifting masks would be domesticated by no one. He attacked the pretentious solemnity of his environment with the weapons of the jokester, as Nietzsche himself, incidentally, was to experience: already after their first meeting he characterized Wagner as a "fabulously spirited and fiery man, who speaks rapidly, is very witty, and can amuse a the most intimate company."[4] His guests often

---

[3] *ibid.*, August 17, 1878.
[4] Dieter Borchmeyer, Jörg Salaquarda, eds., *Nietzsche und Wagner. Stationen einer epochalen Begegnung*, (Ffurt/Leipzig, 1994), v. I, p. 311.

felt themselves in the presence of a force of nature, in which the line between fantasy and reality was blurred—wherever Wagner was, there was theater.

"His whole body," reported the writer Louis de Fourcaud, "was under the control of his nerves, and contained an electricity that communicated itself to his hearers. I can still see him growing restless on his chair, rising, walking back and forth while speaking; I hear him still pouring forth, holding back, growing impatient, breaking out in laughter, interrupting serious thoughts with jocular expressions, jumping from some striking anecdote to lofty ideas. He did not expound in a continuous development on one and the same subject . . . rather [he] delighted in a thousand inspirations."[5]

The question whether this tragic artist, freighted with so much historical and moral baggage, was truly funny, and did not—as Bayreuth tradition would have it—parade through life with grim classical gravity, can be answered unequivocally. He was indeed, and as will be demonstrated, in all twelve keys. There is plenty of laughter even in his stage works. Now quiet, now loud, now mocking, now gloating. At times love's delight "laughs," at times scornful laughter "shrills." And "radiant love," by the logic of paradox, is conjoined to "laughing death."[6]

Many find Wagner himself risible. No artist has ever been more fulsomely derided; none has ever enjoyed wider renown as the butt of jokes. The man of short stature and large head, caricatured by Thomas Mann as

---

[5] Friedrich Glasenapp, *Das Leben Richard Wagners in sechs Büchern dargestellt*, 6 vols., 4th ed., (Leipzig, 1905), v. VI, p. 249.
[6] "Leuchtende Liebe, lachender Tod," *Siegfried*, Act III.

a "snuff-sniffing gnome from Saxony," became the embodiment of pompous self-promotion, and ridiculous conceit. That he himself was a gifted wag would remain unremarked. Nor has it been registered that he juxtaposed the "laughing death" of his heroic couple, Siegfried and Brünnhilde, with its roguish counterpart: "weeping life."[7]

Also scarcely noted is the close relationship between Germany's most ridiculed genius and its arch lampooner: Wagner, the favorite target of every satirist, came to know and revere the master satirist Heinrich Heine in Paris. From the Jewish poet the anti-Semite not only drew the mythological models for many of his stage works, but also learned to write with a well-sharpened pen, and to understand that with it, everything, even the most serious topic, could be joked about.

Like the ironic poet, his admirer too held "nothing sacred," not even himself. So Heine's well-known poem with the ironically pathetic quatrain,

> *"In the wondrous month of May,*
> *When all the buds burst open,*
> *Then in my heart*
> *Did love open too"*[8]

inspired him to compose a parody, in which Wagner poked fun at himself no less than at his adversaries:

> *"In the wondrous month of May*
> *Richard Wagner crawled from his egg;*

---

[7] Cosima Wagner, *op. cit.*, v. II, February 2, 1879.
[8] "*Im wunderschönen Monat Mai,/Als alle Knospen sprangen,/Da ist in meinem Herzen/Die Liebe aufgegangen.*"

Joachim Köhler

*Many of those who love him wish
He'd rather stayed inside it."*[9]

Wagner would not have been Wagner had he not, in his auto-salutation—he was born on May 22, 1813—also concealed an allusion. The "egg" from which he crawled at birth may well have been an allusion to the paternity of his step-father Geyer, whose surname he had borne as a child. "His father was an actor by the name of Geyer," Nietzsche asserted as well, whereby the philosopher implied that his erstwhile idol had been sired in adultery by the man with the bird's name.

Worse, as Nietzsche would have it, "A vulture is nearly an eagle . . .,"[10] as much as to suggest that the anti-Jewish inclined musician himself had Jewish forbears. Although this, like the matter of Geyer's paternity, was a canard, the genealogical insinuation added endless fuel to the quarrel over Wagner. And the quarrel over him knew no bounds. From the outset, the fanaticism of his adversaries—those "many . . . who love him"—was matched by that of his adherents, who displayed a cultish adoration of him and his music.

On this subject, too, the idol satirized himself in another birthday verse:

*"Yes, yes, it was in May,
In fact I myself was there.
They pulled me by my ears,*

---

[9] "*Im wunderschönen Monat Mai/Kroch Richard Wagner aus dem Ei;/Es wünschten Viele die ihn lieben,/er wäre lieber drin geblieben,*" Richard Wagner, *Sämtliche Schriften und Dichtungen,* Volksausgabe, vols. I-XII, and XVI (Leipzig, undated, but 1911), v. XII, p. 374.

[10] Friedrich Nietzsche, *Sämtliche Werke, Kritische Studienausgabe in 15 Bänden,* (KSA), eds., Giorgio Colli & Mazzino Montinari (Munich, 1980), v. VI, p. 41. "Geyer" is the German word for vulture.

Thus was I born a musician."[11]

In contrast to his omnipresent dramas and his treatises (deservedly dismissed in the long run), Wagner's comedic side has remained virtually unknown. Still today, whether he is written, spoken, or argued about, it remains correspondingly a humorless business. The grim seriousness that characterizes every sort of dealing with Wagner seems equally reflected in images of him. Whether crowned with laurels, or being pelted with rotten eggs, he presents the same face, as impervious as the marble from which it is chiseled. One never sees him laughing.

Nor has one tried to picture him laughing: devotees because it would tarnish the picture of their "Master;" critics, because he might—God forbid!—appear human. The wish is to have him just as serious as a venerable classic or a favorite villain. And so both sides have embraced the stern marble portrait the Bayreuth religious cult has given out as the "only true Wagner."

But did such a one ever exist? Those who knew the composer personally have been hard pressed to provide a clear answer. Each time one thought to have glimpsed the "true" Wagner, sooner or later a plethora of opposing personalities have crowded to the fore all claiming to represent the only true Wagner.

Looking at him, said his brother-in-law Emile Ollivier, one saw "the prophet and the joker ... conjoined in his face,"[12] that is, polar opposites as could hardly more

---

[11] Richard Wagner, *op. cit.*, v. XII, p. 374. *"Ja, ja, es war im Mai,/Da war ich auch dabei./Man zog mich bei den Ohren,/Drum bin ich musikalisch geboren."*

[12] Werner Otto, ed., *Richard Wagner. Ein Lebens und Charakterbild in Dokumenten und zeitgenösischen Darstellungen* (Berlin, 1990), p. 38.

starkly be imagined. Again, the director Eduard Devrient spoke of Wagner's "sharp lawyer's face," on which the iconic satin beret "clumsily donned seemed comical."[13] By contrast, Wagner's French admirer Edouard Schuré was reminded of two classical models: seen from the front, Wagner resembled Faust, while in profile he looked like Mephistopheles.[14]

Not without a hint of horror, Wagner's house organ, *Bayreuther Blätter*, once described his "truly demonic gift of transforming himself into all sorts of forms," so that he could "as though with a stroke of magic assume any given character."[15] His admirer Edouard Schuré was also struck by this "demonic" capacity for transmogrification. Wagner amused him once with impressions of his stage heroes: "the black melancholy of the Dutchman, Tannhäuser's unbridled desire, Lohengrin's unapproachable pride, Hagen's icy irony, and Alberich's wrath," as well as "the two poles of his nature, Wotan and Siegfried." And all this through lightning-swift transformation of his facial expression.[16]

Wagner's histrionic talent, with which he consciously mixed a bit of the comic, even a touch of the carnival, toggled between theater and reality, according to his whim, displaying his own manifold sides and simultaneously their interchangeability: as though they were real human beings, he suffered the torments of the dying Tristan and the empathetic Kurvenal, "as though he were each," Cosima movingly recorded.[17] And in

---

[13] Eduard Devrient, *Aus seinen Tagebüchern* (Karlsruhe, 1852-1870; Weimar, 1964), p. 382.
[14] Edouard Schuré, Souvenirs sur Richard Wagner (Paris, 1900), p. 54.
[15] Herbert Bart/Dietrich Mack/Egon Voss, *Richard Wagner, Leben und Werk* (Munich, 1982), p. 461.
[16] Schuré, *op. cit.*, p. 56.
[17] Cosima Wagner, *op. cit.*, v. II, November 7, 1880.

the next moment he displayed the ridiculous poses of social role-playing that reduced his allegedly authentic fellow humans to the level of marionettes.

Once, when he discovered high-ranking officers were among his guests at Wahnfried, he dressed up with a lieutenant-colonel's helmet and a general's sword, drawing the weapon before the assembled company, indeed "with such a playful expression that everyone laughed heartily." Whether the merriment communicated itself to the officers, too, whom their host was teasing, is not recorded.[18]

His multiple personality, which Wagner himself once described as "a mix of Hamlet and Don Quixote,"[19] proved also the despair of the artists who sought to capture him in portraits. In frustration, they had to content themselves with reproducing the mask-like countenance that had become his trademark.

When the husband of Wagner's former beloved Mathilde Wesendonck commissioned an oil portrait of the composer as a gift to mark his wife's happy delivery of a child, the painter Cäsar Willich experienced these same frustrations with the Genius. No sooner had the seasoned portraitist set up his easel in Wagner's luxurious "beaver's nest" in Biebrich on the Rhine and admired the composer's Venetian silk pajamas, than he already ran up against the limits of his art. For the face he was supposed to capture was nowhere to be seen, and each sketch had to be corrected, because in the meantime the subject, whose humorous vein was unknown to Willich, had assumed a different look.

---

[18] Sophie Rützow, *Richard Wagner und Bayreuth* (Munich, 1943), p. 156.
[19] Cosima Wagner, *op. cit.*, v. II, August 7, 1878.

One picture after another was roughed out and discarded at once," an eye-witness recalled, "because the subject brought an entirely altered facial expression from one sitting to the next. The unfortunate painter was beside himself, and once confessed to me: 'In the whole of my practice I have never experienced a similar case. Mr. Wagner makes a different face every day.'"[20] How the beautiful Mathilde, immortalized by Wagner as opera's Isolde, reacted to the portrait is unknown. The depicted subject himself declared it an "awful picture."[21]

The sculptor Gustav Adolph Kietz, who was to fashion the bust of the Master for "Wahnfried," the residence of Wagner's later years, scarcely had better luck. Kietz too was confronted, as a visitor noted, with the "very mercurial facial expressions" of the subject, whereby "each expression reflected his emotional state with lightning speed."[22]

Once, when the artist raised his eyes from his clay model, he saw "to his horror a terrible grimace with distorted eyes, the mouth stretched wide open with both fingers."[23] Though Wagner may have stopped short of sticking out his tongue, his admirer Kietz seems to have gotten the message: within the elegantly attired shell of the universal genius lurked a clown, who shrank from no buffoonery. Or had he wished to demonstrate graphically that he was not to be confused with his death-mask?

---

[20] Wendelin Weißheimer, *Erlebnisse mit Richard Wagner, Franz Liszt und vielen anderen Zeitgenossen* (Stuttgart, 1898), p. 128.
[21] Richard Wagner, *Mein Leben 1813-1868*. Vollständige, kommentierte Ausgabe, Martin Gregor-Dellin, ed. (Munich/Leipzig, 1994), p. 706.
[22] Adolph Kohut, *Der Meister von Bayreuth* (Berlin, 1905), p. 184.
[23] Erich Kloss, *Wagner-Anekdoten* (Leipzig, 1908), p. 120.

The man who liked to make faces both at his contemporaries and at posterity, also composed his own epitaph—one hardly in line with the expectations of his admirers. Nor did it actually make its way onto his gravestone:

"Here lies Wagner, who came to nothing,
not even knight of the shabbiest order;
couldn't coax a dog from behind the oven,
let alone a doctorate from the academy."[24]

The rhymester breaks off here—his self-composed epitaph remaining (in the *Meistersinger* fashion) a fragment. Nor was it seriously meant, for he never cared about public honors: he ridiculed laurel wreaths; he made use of an exotic medal he had received as a prop in his puppet theater; and when offered an honorary doctorate, he politely declined. Even with respect to the dogs, the epitaph had it wrong: they readily came out from behind the oven, for in those four-legged creatures, the composer elicited extraordinarily sympathetic feelings, which he happily reciprocated. In the garden at Wahnfried where he lies today, his dogs also lie buried.

No, it was never meant seriously—this epitaph. And it was precisely this that was the message to the reader, the well-disposed as well as the averse: that all things relating to Wagner were not quite so seriously intended as Wagnerites and anti-Wagnerites alike would have it.

Dear admirer and detractor (it as much as said), dear congregations of both worshipers and poisoners! I am

---

[24] Wagner, *Sämtliche Schriften und Dichtungen*, v. XII, p. 368. *"Hier liegt Wagner, der nichts geworden,/nicht einmal Ritter vom lupigsten Orden;/nicht einen Hund hinterem Ofen entlockt er,/Universitäten nicht mal 'nen Dokter."*

not the person you think me. Moreover the person I *am*, you do not know. Besides, I am firmly convinced "that no one can seriously hate me unless he is mistaken about me—which, in the end, awakens my sense of humor and so affords me the only joy I am capable of."[25]

---

[25] Richard Wagner, *Sämtliche Briefe* (Leipzig & Wiesbaden, 1967-2000), p. 206.

Act One

"A Kind of Mad Genius"

*"Were I a numbskull, I wouldn't be Wagner,
for Wagners are quite brilliant people all,
as one can see already in 'Faust.'"*[26]

Scene 1

"A Cherub from Olympic Regions"

At more or less the same time mankind realized its dream of speaking across long-distances and traveling by horseless carriage, Richard Wagner, too, fulfilled a lifelong dream—of a theater in which only his own name appeared on the program. Just as farfetched an idea that in the future the ordinary citizen would possess a telephone and an automobile, was the thought that an artist might own a stage on which only his own works would be presented. Nearly everyone who heard of it was in agreement with Kaiser Wilhelm I, who confessed to him, "I never thought you could bring it off."[27]

---

[26] Cosima Wagner, *Diaries*, October 2, 1878. "*Wäre ich ein Schafskopf, hieße ich nicht Wagner,/denn alle Wagners sind besonders geniale Leute,/wie man schon im 'Faust' sehen kann.*" Wagner's self-irony is based on Goethe's characterization of his fictional Wagner, Faust's pupil, as a narrow-minded pedant, whose sole ambition is worldly honor.

[27] Martin Gregor-Dellin, *Richard Wagner. Sein Leben—Sein Werk—Sein Jahrhundert*, (Munich, 1980), p. 716.

But bring it off he did. In 1876, the year Alexander Graham Bell invented the telephone and August Otto his eponymous motor, Wagner opened an opera house the likes of which the world had never known. Built on a rise overlooking Bayreuth, it resembled a barn more than a show-piece of the foundational era of imperial Germany; in place of pillars and a façade decorated with classical figures in relief, one saw only brick walls held together with wooden beams.

Plain as the exterior may have been, its interior was in equal measure revolutionary. In the seating area, the architect had done away with the strict class divisions prevailing in theaters world-wide. Apart from the "Prince's Gallery" for Wagner's patron King Ludwig II, neither boxes nor plush seats were provided for the aristocracy and the well-to-do. Everyone had to endure the same hard seats, and stoically sweat out the four-part *Ring of the Nibelung*. Had Wagner had his way it would, moreover, have been free. For this gas-lit world novelty that seemed to underscore his legendary egotism, was actually conceived as a people's theater, in which freedom, equality, and fraternity were intended to reign—with Wagner's art as its mythological underpinnings.

A year before, the festival artists had streamed in from every part of Germany to rehearse the *Ring of the Nibelung*. This music drama, which took up an entire evening and three half days, was, according to Wagner's wishes, to be the only work presented here. He had propagated his dream project for a quarter of a century—intriguing the press, mobilizing friends, fascinating the King of Bavaria, and finally—thanks to the canny town fathers who promoted his project because his project promoted Bayreuth—triumphing over every obstacle in his way.

Before the start of the first *Ring* rehearsal, the singers had all taken their places in the classless rows of seats, in a festive mood at the unusual occasion and in anticipatory delight over the 62-year old master from whom (since he loved speaking, and at length) they expected a speech equal to the occasion. Years before he had predicted of his theater that every visitor would "attain to a heretofore unknown insight," which would "ignite a light that would reveal to him things of which he had no idea before."[28]

"I never thought you could have brought it off." In this caricature from the Vienna *Floh*, Kaiser Wilhelm I bestows an over-sized carnival-medal on the Bayreuth theater-sovereign.

---

[28] Richard Wagner, *Dichtungen und Schriften*, Jubiläumsausgabe in zehn Bänden, (Frankfurt, 1983), v. III, p. 357.

Just as eager on that hot June day in 1875 was the public, waiting to applaud the man whose highly improbable life's dream had now come to fruition. The murmur of the crowd stilled, and from out of the dark offstage, a small figure appeared, stepping quickly towards the orchestra pit, balancing himself on the plank spanning the meter-deep abyss, coming finally to rest on the apron. It was he, the "Master," though dressed not, as expected, in his legendary get-up of silk and satin, but rather in a linen smock, a professorial pince-nez perched on his nose, the famous oversized beret aslant his head, and a colorful handkerchief hanging from his pocket as though he had just indulged in a pinch of snuff.

Though all eyes were on him, not a sound escaped his lips. He stood, silent, looking serenely at the audience, which returned his gaze. When the tension had become nearly unbearable, something occurred of which no one could "have had the least premonition," perhaps not even he himself. With the grace of a ballerina, the little man threw his arms up, and with his upper body leaning forward, lifted one leg perpendicularly and remained so for a moment, "imitating the pose of a hovering genius."

This lasted until the comic nature of the situation dawned on the audience, whereupon, as someone present on the occasion recalled, "the general astonishment and delight was great."[29] And many among the notables and sponsors, musicians and technicians, disciples and critics seem even to have realized that the venerable theater director had held a

---

[29] Otto, p. 527.

mirror up to them: "you wish to see a genius? Please—here he is!"

The *Ring*-poet had always felt a kinship to the legendary Till Eulenspiegel, who laughingly showed people their own stupidity. As a fledgling composer during the *Rienzi* period, he was—as one singer recounted—enamored "of the craziest Eulenspiegel pranks." "He donned all sorts of disguises, crawled under the table, imitated a barking dog, and indulged in other monkeyshines of the sort."[30] Even when no one understood what the artist intended with his mad antics, he nonetheless had the laughers always on his side, though they could never be quite sure whether he was laughing with them or at them.

Decades later, when he held court with his beloved Cosima von Bülow in Munich, Wagner, now world famous, still had not given up his taste for Eulenspiegel-like pranks. With mischievous glee, according to his disciple Peter Cornelius, he "played the clown," and that "to the entertainment of all, with the exception of Frau von Bülow, who disapproved such low amusements. But Wagner went on with his games notwithstanding. He crawled under the piano, jumped onto the piano," and relished in giving impressions of well-known personalities. At the conclusion he read aloud a poem of praise written in his honor, peppered "with improvised mis-readings, for which he had a great talent"—as Beckmesser's grotesque "Prize Song" in *Die Meistersinger* amply demonstrates.[31]

Only those unaware of the original genesis of the *Ring* might find this incompatible with the lofty image of the

---

[30] Kohut, p. 31.
[31] Carl Maria Cornelius, *Peter Cornelius*, (Regensburg, 1925), v. II, p. 63.

Nibelung composer. It was not the legendary dragon-slayer Siegfried, but rather that terror of the bourgeoisie, the cunning Till Eulenspiegel from whom Wagner took the germinal idea for his universal drama. Stranded at Travemünde in 1837, in a sailor's tavern the peripatetic composer came across the folkloric book *Till Eulenspiegel*, about the adventures of a character known for unmasking people as fools, dressed in the mask of a fool himself.

In the course of his reading at Travemünde, Wagner hit "upon the idea of a genuinely German comic opera . . . When years later I finally sketched out the poem of my 'Young Siegfried' — I recall — memories of this melancholy sojourn at Travemünde and of my reading of the 'Eulenspiegel' were once more vividly awakened in me."[32]

It was not just the bloody *Ring*-tragedy of theft of gold and global immolation that had its birth in comedy. The career of its musico-dramatic creator began under a comedic sign. Wagner may have been alluding to just that when he mimed the hovering genius for his Bayreuth audience. The affected pose in which he poked fun at this provisional summit in his career, namely, had its origins — as he reveals in his memoir — in his earliest beginnings. Not coincidentally, after reading *Mein Leben*, Friedrich Nietzsche observed that "Richard Wagner's life contains a good deal of comedy, and remarkably grotesque at that."[33]

Among Wagner's youthful Dresden reminiscences is an elemental scene in which alongside the little Richard Geyer, several key figures from his childhood take part:

---

[32] Wagner, *Mein Leben*, p. 153.
[33] Nietzsche, *KSA*, v. I, p. 441.

The Laughing Wagner

in honor of Friedrich August, King of Saxony (whom Wagner's late father had served in his capacity as police official), the comedy *The Vineyard on the Elbe*, for which Carl Maria von Weber omposed a score, was performed. The famous court Kapellmeister in turn was a friend of Wagner's step-father (or father), Ludwig Geyer, who not only acted in the piece, but brought his four-year-old stepson (or son) Richard onstage with him—less out of affection, than because the large family needed urgently to better its financial circumstances.

Interpolated throughout the comedy, the royal family was entertained with images from Greek vases in the form of "living pictures," in which actors assumed frozen poses representing scenes from classical mythology. In one of these, the four-year-old "appeared," as he later recounted, "as an angel sewn entirely into a knit suit, with wings on [his] back, in an arduously rehearsed graceful pose." Apparently, he portrayed the genius, listed in the libretto as "a cherub from Olympic regions," so convincingly that following the performance he received a "large sugar pretzel, which I was assured had been awarded me by the King personally."[34]

This was not the only reason this son of a policeman (or of an actor) believed he had a more than superficial affinity with the aristocracy. Only a chosen few were initiate to the legend (which he chose to believe since it buttressed his sense of personal mission) that his mother had been the issue of an adulterous liaison between a beautiful baker's wife from Weissenfels and Konstanin, Crown Prince of Saxony—which would automatically have elevated her son Richard to the

---

[34] Wagner, *Mein Leben*, p. 11

ranks of European high aristocracy. Only decades after Wagner's death was the whole story revealed to have been an embarrassing misunderstanding: his mother, Rosine, had been not the daughter but rather the mistress of the Prince, abandoned by him with a small settlement in Leipzig long before Richard's birth.

And in Leipzig, Richard was born into the hustle and bustle of a large bohemian family, surrounded by seven musically ambitious siblings, in the charge of mother, Rosine, her husband, Friedrich, and the family friend Ludwig Geyer, brilliant not only as an actor, but also as painter, poet, and puppeteer. The apartment building in which the extended family lived, "the House of the Red and White Lions," carried on its doorway the titular decorative stone lions, whose colors, according to Wagner, gained their true significance only with his birth: "The white lion turned red with fury, and the red, white with fear."[35] When later he was offered the purchase of this ramshackle birth house, he replied roguishly that he no longer had a need for it since he could "not be born a second time."[36]

Wagner's later assertion that he had grown up "completely feral" like his hero Siegfried flowed from the nature of the comic actor's household: costumes were constantly being tried on, masks exchanged, and songs rehearsed, by means of which his sisters Rosalie, Luise, Clara, Ottilie, and Cäcilie contributed from an early age to the family coffers. In the wake of the early death of Police Official Wagner money was scarce all around, so they were put onto the stage by Geyer as soon as they could walk.

---

[35] Cosima Wagner, *Diaries*, October 13, 1879.
[36] *Ibid.*, May 2, 1881.

Geyer himself appeared in comedies as well as horror dramas, in which as Knight of the Dragon's Rock in *The Devil's Mill on Wienerberg* for example he made the unsophisticated audience tremble and thrill with fear. He titled the best known of his own comedies in a comic-horror vein *The Massacre of the Innocents of Bethlehem*. In spite of their collective industry, the family was unable to get ahead. In self-mockery, Geyer presented his Rosine with a cake, "on which stood a little man who," in Cosima's coy diary formulation, "was passing a ducat."[37]

Three years after his silent role as winged genius, Richard would celebrate his next stage triumph, this time with spoken lines. In Schiller's *William Tell*, in which Geyer appeared as the rogue Gessler, he played a son of the hero. At the premiere, in the scene in which Tell with his older son (played by the sister Clara) takes his leave of the family, Richard, according to the script, was supposed to say, "And I stay with mother." Having suddenly forgotten the line, in his distress he cried out what was on his mind in any case, "Clara, you're going; I want to come along too!" and vanished behind the scenery. The audience, grateful for the unexpected, applauded "enthusiastically, so that little Richard thereby enjoyed his first triumph on the Dresden Court Stage."[38]

It may well be that the young Wagner took from this experience the lesson that would characterize his artistic creation henceforth: whoever seeks success must defy convention, preferably with wit, but with force if necessary. Only he can win over an audience who astonishes, even ambushes it, and is never at a loss

---

[37] *Ibid.*, November 9, 1882.
[38] Otto, p. 8.

for a retort. Once, when schoolboy Wagner was caught not having prepared his lesson, he claimed to have a "major role" in a play by Kotzebue that he had been obliged to learn—in question was the popular drama *Menschenhaß und Reue*. Asked for the name of the play, which had slipped his mind, he improvised: "Menschen außer der Reihe,"[39] a remark that was met with his teacher's laughter, whereby he had pointedly characterized his family's circumstances.

These bit parts on the Dresden stage were not equal to his need to perform. He wanted to "act" not only in the theater but as much as possible in life too. When at the age of five he attended the opera for the first time, where a grizzly piece about Bluebeard was being given, he couldn't rest until once more at home he could impersonate the serial killer. "A home-made paper helmet on [his] head," he performed for his family the big aria "Ha! Du Falsche! Die Türe offen!"[40] His histrionic passion helped him rise above their derisive amusement, and spurred him on to further operatic performance. In the children's room, he produced repeated performances of Weber's hit drama *Der Freischütz*, for whose wolf's glen scene he fashioned gloomy papier-mâché sets and a wild boar on rollers, and, in the demonic leading role, drove the casting of the bullets to its midnight climax.

Richard liked to surprise his family with his own puppet-theater productions, though they did not

---

[39] Wagner, *Mein Leben*, p. 12. "Menschenhaß und Reue" may be translated as "Misanthropy and Repentance," but the play is known in English as "The Stranger." Wagner's improvised title, which comes across as something of a punning travesty, "Menschen außer der Reihe," may be translated as "People acting unconventionally."

[40] *Ibid.*, p. 238. "Ha! You false one! Throw open the doors!"

always turn out to be triumphs. One tragedy, on the theme of the wife-murderer Bluebeard, for which he secretly carved figures and sewed costumes, inadvertently came to light even before its "dazzling performance." "After I had sketched out the first scene," he reported, "my sisters discovered the manuscript and subjected it to immoderate ridicule: the fearful lover's line, 'Already I hear the knight trotting' was, to my great chagrin, eternally recited to me with sham pathos."[41]

"Because he was so sensitive," noted Cosima, the youngster was given the rather demeaning nickname "Bailiff Scrambled Egg."[42] Once in school, the whiny problem child evolved into class-clown. One of his specialties was imitating the teacher; to get a hearing he would jump onto the teacher's desk. Admonished by the butt of his satire, he knew how to wriggle out so artfully that, "nonplussed by his improvisations,"[43] the teacher would waive punishment.

Authority figures of all sorts seem to have been a red flag to the boy; not even the clergy were immune. The child who once, "in ecstatic enthusiasm, [had] wished to take the place of the redeemer on the cross" before which an impassioned populace had fallen to their knees, now as a candidate for confirmation picked out the clergy as special target of his jokes. He confessed to Cosima that he had so lost respect for his pastor at that time "that he not unwillingly joined in mockery of him,

---

[41] *Ibid.*, p. 19.
[42] Cosima Wagner, *Diaries*, January 11, 1870. "Amtmann Rührei" involves a pun on "rühren," which means both to stir—as in scrambled eggs—and to touch or move emotionally.
[43] *Ibid.*, March 11, 1878.

and in collusion with his fellow candidates even ate up a part of his penitent's offering in sweets."[44]

Skillful in the effects to which all comedians owe their success, the young Wagner had already won over the laughers—a talent he retained up to his death. No one told an anecdote better, or delivered the punchline of a joke more trenchantly. But he was also prey to the secret anxiety of so many comedians: of being unwittingly funny. Even when they mean to be serious, they sometimes provoke laughter. From there to ridiculous is but a short step, and often a well-teased audience belatedly takes its revenge in disparaging the jokester.

Even the young Richard virtually invited this scenario. Involuntarily, he provoked general snickering and presented to the victims of his whims the soft spot they could ridicule. For he was in fact the "little" Richard, and remained so his whole life. Only his head, it seems, proved the exception to the refusal of the rest of his body to grow, reaching normal size, but which in association with his fineness of limb appeared disproportional. The music critic Theodor W. Adorno, no giant himself, wrote that Wagner had "narrowly escaped the image of a dwarf."[45]

"The large, silken-haired head with the blue eyes"—as biographer Martin Gregor-Dellin visualized the child— "sat atop a far too puny body, with short, spindly little legs."[46] Wagner's delicacy, possibly the sequela of childhood diseases, proved a handicap, but motivated him on the other hand to extraordinary efforts. To

---
[44] Wagner, *Mein Leben*, p. 27.
[45] Theodor W. Adorno, *Versuch über Wagner*, (Munich, 1964), p. 21.
[46] Gregor-Dellin, p. 24.

compete with those larger than himself — which is to say everyone — he had to achieve greater things. And because the stunted boy was always a nose-length ahead of the others intellectually, he out-distanced them in the realm where size doesn't matter.

Scene 2

A Man Stands on his Head

The stark fear of simply being overlooked may have triggered in the small Richard that penchant for extravagant dress which he cultivated from early on. When his god-father, the merchant Adolf Träger, made the twelve-year-old a present of "one of his blue-gray tail coats and a red Turkish waistcoat," he contributed these to the ample wardrobe of the family, "over which Richard's mother laughed heartily."[47] With him, it seems, things rarely ended without laughter. When he was emulating the Paris dandies in his late twenties, his amused portraitist Friedrich Pecht described him as "despite his all too short legs, [a] remarkably elegant, even distinguished young man."[48] Dressed grandly, no one ever seems small.

The same is true of him who achieves great things. From his "earliest childhood," as Wagner revealed, within him "the thought dwelt [of wishing to be] something great." "He recalled once having written a friend inviting him to visit and undertake a joint reading about the deeds of the great Napoleon,"[49] the

---

[47] Cosima Wagner, *Diaries*, January 9, 1870.
[48] Friedrich Pecht, *Aus meiner Zeit*, (Munich, 1894), p. 203.
[49] Cosima Wagner, *Diaries*, April 1, 1872.

"great" Napoleon, who showed the world that physical size and historical greatness occasionally stand inversely related to one another.

And how tall was Wagner in actuality? While his admirers measured him at 1.66 meters (Martin Gregor-Dellin), his detractors allowed just 1.53 meters (Robert Gutmann), which goes to show that faith, though unable perhaps to move mountains, can nonetheless influence our perception of height. Take your pick, in other words. In the case of Napoleon too, by the way, whose various measurements resembled Wagner's. According to the estimation of Wagner's friend Emma Herwegh, who described him as a "pocket edition of a man,"[50] it was purely a matter of roguish malice.

However one assesses his physical size, impossible to ignore was the singular disparity between his dainty body and the giant head atop it. It was this disproportionality, too, that earned his appearance the reputation of the dwarflike, which he certainly knew how to compensate for by the grandiosity of his projected self. The comic effect remained in either case. It occurred to one thoroughly well-meaning if somewhat punctilious observer only a year before Wagner's death "that his appearance did not correspond to his gargantuan works! To be sure his remarkable head with its protruding forehead bespoke enormous strength of will and unbending energy, but his tiny body did not correspond to the picture one would have conjured up of the creator of these gods and heroes!"[51]

---

[50] Julius Kapp, *Wagner und die Frauen*, (Berlin, 1951), p. 111.
[51] Felix Philippi, *Münchner Bilderbogen*, (Berlin, 1912), p. 116.

The Laughing Wagner

Little man with large head. A Viennese caricaturist captured Wagner's bow at a concert address.

The conventional dictum that "size doesn't matter" is admirably exemplified by Wagner: how quickly one forgot his seeming physical inferiority when he could demonstrate the strength and agility that lay in this body. Already as a student he astonished his fellows with dare-devil flights onto school roofs or performed gymnastic feats that—and this he valued most— "no one could copy."

Inspired by acrobats and tight-rope walkers, to be seen at any marketplace of the time, the young scholar secretly practiced the break-neck feats that left his comrades in awe. The success he aimed at with such exhibitions earned him a reputation as clown, acrobat, and daredevil climber—a reputation he never afterwards wished to relinquish. Feats the ten-year-old gymnast had performed for his class still thrilled his audience forty years later in Moscow, where, "warmed with red wine and in the best of moods [he] skillfully demonstrated gymnastic routines," in which "the fifty-year-old [composer] even leapt over a table, which added greatly to the mirth of the assembled company."[52]

Even as a sixty-year-old, he performed his acrobatic arts at Wahnfried, to the delight of his friends and the horror of his wife, who tried everything to prevent her divine husband from risking both limb and reputation. She pleaded fervently with her guests not to encourage him in these disconcerting whims, as for instance when he "climbed trees—confirmed by another source, too—with monkey-like agility."[53] "I beg you," she whispered to an American visitor, who, breathless with excitement, was watching him climb a tree, "don't look at him; it only encourages him to take even greater risks."[54] The thrill his dare-devil feats evoked dissolved into relieved laughter and applause as soon as they reached their successful conclusion. The looming tragedy proved in the end a comedy of showmanship.

Whatever he dreamed up for his audience always entailed risk. Whenever the opportunity presented

---

[52] Otto, p. 286.
[53] *Ibid.*, p. 387.
[54] H. R. Haweis, *My Musical Memories*, (New York, 1884), p. 180.

The Laughing Wagner

itself, he climbed aloft. Since trees alone weren't enough for him, he excelled as a climber of building facades. For example in a hotel one night he "climbed along the outer ledge on the second floor of the building wall from one window to the other," which, as he proudly reported, "naturally horrified those unfamiliar with my penchant for acrobatic acts, developed in earliest boyhood."[55] That the young man was inebriated at the time seems to have enhanced the thrill.

He relished the fine art of scaling statues too. At the time of his *Lohengrin*, when he was living in an old Dresden palace, he received visitors not at his apartment door, but in the garden, where he would climb a larger-than-life statue group. Mounted "on Neptune's neck,"[56] he could wave to his arriving guests from afar.

He climbed horizontally as well. In 1860, when Wagner put on *Tannhäuser* in Paris, the famous choreographer Lucien Petipa was struck by his unconventional manner of accessing the orchestra pit. Instead of using the aisle, he balanced his way across the parterre seats. According to Petipa, he stepped from his place "at the rear of the hall, across the seats, walking on his hands as well as his feet, even at the risk of fracturing arms and legs."[57] Inspecting the Bayreuth theater, whose bare shell had just been completed, Wagner climbed "like a cat up to the uppermost height of the scaffolding. All eyes," according to construction

---

[55] Wagner, *Mein Leben*, p. 93.
[56] *Ibid.*, p. 357.
[57] Otto, p. 237.

foreman Runkwitz, "followed him anxiously, but for myself my heart was in my throat. Had he fallen!"[58]

The fact that he had so often performed "over the abyss," yet had never fallen, must have contributed to his enormous self-confidence in seeking to conquer ever new heights. Like his hero Siegfried, he shrank from no danger, and proved to everyone that he, as no one else, had "not learned fear," or — for that matter — respect for the "politically correct." Let the bourgeoisie sneer at his demonstrative otherness — like Till Eulenspiegel, he stuck out his tongue at them.

Not coincidentally, he loved to portray his "topsy-turvy world" in the form of a head-stand. He had been executing this acrobatic number since childhood, indeed on whatever surface came to hand. "Wagner," recalled Wendelin Weissheimer of the days of the Munich *Tristan*, "showed off suddenly during a rehearsal as a brilliant head-stander. Everyone had to laugh when, in the midst of Miss Deinet's (Brangäne's) singing he suddenly braced his head on the sofa and stretched his legs up in the air against the wall."[59] In the ensuing decade, his efforts to amuse the cast with head-stands during the *Nibelungen* rehearsals, led to some embarrassment.[60] These surprising interludes were traced to Wagner's predilection for Champagne, which — as was widely known — was sent him by the case personally by his friend, Monsieur Chandon.

A certain garden table Wagner had chosen as pad for his gymnastic exhibitions at the time of the *Tristan* production in Vienna presented him with a special

---

[58] *Ibid.*, p. 471.
[59] Weißheimer, p. 338.
[60] Kloss, p. 21.

challenge. While guests at his villa in Penzing philosophized about the wonders of his art, the composer stepped out into the garden unremarked, from where he called to the assembled company that out here they would have their true wonder. "When the ladies and gentlemen had stepped out onto the terrace, this sight greeted them: Richard Wagner in a head-stand, employing a white-painted garden table as his platform, arms and legs balanced skillfully."[61]

No doubt he achieved the pinnacle of his acrobatic daring in Biebrich on the Rhine while impatiently awaiting the arrival of his stars, the married singers, Ludwig and Malwine Schnorr von Carolsfeld, with whom he was to rehearse his latest music-drama *Tristan und Isolde*. "On their approach, already from afar the Schnorrs could see the Master on the look out from the balcony, where he paced back and forth, scanning the street up and down to catch sight of his guests, just arrived by train. Scarcely had he spotted them when, at a distance and with lively gestures of delight he greeted them. Then—suddenly!—he swung himself in a single bound onto one of the vases, and, head down, legs in the air, waved with these, to the great horror of his guests, verging on the edge of the balcony in this precarious position for a period of several seconds, saluting to and fro."[62]

Picture the scene: two widely renowned opera stars, the tragic roles of Tristan and Isolde swirling in their heads, come upon the no less famous composer of these roles, standing on his head on a vase high above the street, waving with his skinny legs. Seized with "greatest terror," they rush up the steps to restore him

---

[61] Otto, p. 256.
[62] Glasenapp, v.III, p. 380.

to solid ground. And what is it he wishes to convey to them? That he stands on his head out of sheer delight? That he stands everything previously thought of as art on its head? That, to achieve his goals, he will risk everything, including his own life? Or just that he wants to show what he can do apart from merely composing *Tristan und Isolde*?

The little man with the big head seems to have made it his life's mission not to be ignored. He succeeded in this even with his caricaturists: no other artist was so often the butt of jokes—the result not only of his appearance itself, but also of the sheer recognize-ability of his features, which could be captured even by only moderately talented draftsmen. But as to whether this flood of derisive images, which filled whole volumes, ever struck home with their object himself—no record exists that this otherwise voluble speaker ever uttered a word.

Scene 3

The Nose of God

Wagner's intentional humor was always also attended by the unintentional. Even as a child, he had experienced the double edge of "everyone laughs at me," and not just because, having brought others to laughter, he was later smiled at himself. As it were gratuitously, to his outward appearance—which lacked physical majesty to begin with—was attached an illness that at irregular intervals occasioned risible disfigurement.

All his life, Wagner suffered from erysipelas, a common variant of shingles, which is heralded by depression, and causes facial redness and swelling accompanied by fever. This infirmity, surprising to the un-afflicted, highly embarrassing to the afflicted, represents a severe test precisely for someone who, like Wagner, seeks to project a *bella figura*, especially since by neither pharmaceutical nor cosmetic means was he able to overcome it.

Wagner bore it with grim humor. Plagued during the conception of *Tristan* with his ever-recurring erysipelas, he unburdened himself to his friend Liszt in these words: "To add to the thorns of my existence, now the 'roses' have bloomed for me too."[63] On another occasion, he was reminded of Shakespeare's *Midsummer Night's Dream*, the role of Bottom transformed into an ass-like grotesque falling to him.[64] In fact he awoke often enough with swollen cheeks and a bulbous nose, at which his family—half embarrassed, half amused—marveled as at a natural wonder.

During these attacks he was particularly depressed over having to renounce, on doctor's orders, one of his great passions: snuff. Not coincidentally Thomas Mann referred to him as a "snuff-taking gnome."[65] With self-ironical candor he conceded, "snuff-taking is actually my soul." Cosima in turn found this "very droll,"[66] though not relinquishing her aversion to the habit.

The whole ritual was amusing: in Wagner's rendition, from tapping the pinch out onto the back of his hand and the noisy snort into the nostril, right up to the

---

[63] Wagner, *Sämtliche Briefe*, v. VII, p. 315. "Roses" here is a pun on the German for erysipelas, *Gesichtsrose*.
[64] Cosima Wagner, *Diaries*, December 10, 1879.
[65] Thomas Mann, *Wagner und unsere Zeit*, (Frankfurt, 1983), p. 30.
[66] Cosima Wagner, *Diaries*, January 24, 1883.

explosive discharge with the gun-powder-like blackening of the nose, wiped thoroughly clean with an over-sized handkerchief, the whole process took on the air of the naturally comic. Even if this habit, commonly regarded as plebeian, did not quite accord with the image of the great genius—not to mention his wife's disdain, whose tobacco consumption was limited to cigarettes—he indulged in it to the point of addiction.

"Snuff-taking is actually my soul." When Anton Bruckner visited Bayreuth in 1873, Wagner invited him to sample from his snuff-box. Silhouette by Otto Böhler.

During the composition of *Tristan und Isolde* in Venice, he was able to master the enormous strain thanks only to equally enormous quantities of snuff which he, by his own admission, "used by the pound." As a special mark of favor, others were invited to sample his treasure. A silhouette shows Anton Bruckner bent over

Wagner's snuff-box. And the Bayreuth rehearsals were not the first time he had had a "large red handkerchief"[67] hanging demonstratively from his coat pocket. After a week of medically prescribed abstinence, the slave to the snuff demon lamented that without a pinch he felt "as though [he] would go mad!"[68]

That often happened. Of all times, tormented by erysipelas when he needed his drug the most, the snuff-box was on doctor's orders locked away. Strict bed rest was imposed then, and Wagner was compelled to marshal all his reserves of good humor to get through the experience that drove him crazy when his nose, by his own report, swelled "like a hippopotamus."[69]

Once, when his Bayreuth physician, Dr. Landgraf, prescribed inhalation of marsh-mallow tea vapors, the patient suffered so much from the "powerfully" rising vapors that a strong headache set in. Thereupon the doctor advised the use of a simple paper funnel to direct the steam precisely onto the nose, shielding the rest of his face. The construction of the device itself so impressed the suffering patient that he suggested "sending the paper-cone to the next world's fair for exhibition." When this method actually proved effective, he was utterly enthusiastic, and "called the paper cone the nose of God in contrast to [colloquialisms like] the finger of God or the eye of God."[70]

---

[67] Angelo Neumann, *Erinnerungen an Richard Wagner*, (Leipzig, 1907), p. 4.
[68] Glasenapp, v. VI, p. 291.
[69] Cosima Wagner, *Diaries*, November 11, 12, 1879.
[70] Glasenapp, v. VI, p. 278.

Just as in theology God requires his opposite number, the demonic character of his inhalation aid soon dawned on Wagner. Now he believed he recognized the "devil Nasias" in the "nose of God," which directed hot vapors into his respiratory organ, in allusion "to the evil spirit in the Wartburg contest."[71] Indeed, in E. T. A. Hoffmann's story, "The Singer's Contest" ("*Der Kampf der Sänger*"), which had once inspired Wagner to his *Tannhäuser*, a demon named Nasias appears as a fire-snorting spirit from hell able to alter his size at will—therein resembling Wagner's nose as well as his fictional dwarf/giant Alberich.

After Dr. Landgraf's magic funnel had proven effective for a period of time, the erysipelas took a new tack. This time the doctor prescribed "ice-compresses," which lulled the patient into a light slumber, and inspired interesting dreams. Once, he saw himself transformed into a "Turkish lady, being carried on a litter." Another time, he saw himself as the spouse of the "rosy-fingered dawn" ("*Rhododaktylos Eos*"), and dubbed himself accordingly with the honorific "*Rhodonasilos Tithonos*," the "rosy-nosed Tithonos,"[72] an inspiration ingenious also because although Tithonos—thanks to the intervention of his divine wife— had been granted eternal life by Zeus, he had not been granted eternal youth, because the "rosy-fingered" had neglected to ask for it too. Thus, with advancing age, her poor spouse became ever more dwarf-like, shriveling at last to a keening cricket.

Among the various side effects of Wagner's erysipelas, which as a man in the public eye he feared his whole life, he suffered from hyper-sensitivity of the skin,

---

[71] *Ibid.*, p. 283.
[72] *Ibid.*, p. 286.

compelling him to extravagant choices in the composition of his wardrobe. "The evil of his skin disease," credibly reported his admirer Ferdinand Praeger (other of his Wagner experiences are discredited by embellishment), "permitted him to wear nothing but silk against his naked body. Even touching merely cotton with his hands provoked a shudder through his entire body. For this reason, all the pockets in his clothes were silk, as were the linings. This occasioned a comic scene at the Regent Street shop of a tailor, a German-speaking Pole who thought this luxury unnecessary, so that he assured the composer that 'even the wealthiest people and lords employed only cotton for this purpose, since it was, after all, out of sight.'" Whereupon Wagner, making light of the tailor's naiveté, burst out with irony, "Yes, yes, such is the spirit of the times, everything is mere gold foil, as false as fashion, as Geibel said of the grave: 'Flowers on the outside, all woe within!'"[73]

Aside from the extreme irritability of his skin, which forced him to wear the finest silk underwear (nor did he eschew ladies' negligées), the illness, he was convinced, inflicted a further peculiarity: he was compelled to go through life with virtually no eyebrows. Though he lamented this on aesthetic grounds, the shortcoming did inspire him to witticisms. When his sister Cäcilie, reported to him "horrified" in 1853 that the Dresden police had renewed the wanted poster issued for his

---

[73] Ferdinand Praeger, *Wagner, wie ich ihn kannte*, (Leipzig, 1892), p. 264. The author, who in fact knew Wagner well, has been shown to have indulged in numerous fabrications and falsifications, and therefore even his authentic reminiscences fall under general suspicion. That he has been thoroughly exiled from the Wagner literature, however, may ensue from the fact that his *partially* fictional portrait of Wagner comes nearer the reality—including its comic aspects—than those of his court biographers. In any case, my citation here is with reservations.

arrest as a revolutionary in 1849, complete with a current picture of him, he asked her to greet the police "respectfully" on his behalf, but inform them that the likeness was incorrect: he "now wore long curls, and had very beautifully arched eyebrows."[74]

What he experienced as a painful defect, Cosima transmuted into one of the mosaic stones in her godlike portrait of him. "That he has virtually no eyebrows," she explained, "seems to me like the total absence of the animal nature in his being."[75] The involuntarily transfigured one himself, on the other hand, admired in others — not without irony to be sure — the *presence* of the animalistic. "My God, if I had eyebrows like that, I'd be quite a different fellow,"[76] he once remarked, blinking, and even in advanced age regarding the bushy eyebrows of his otherwise rather timid assistant Wolzogen, one had to believe — he opined — a person with those could turn the world upside-down, while he, Wagner, was "energy itself, yet had none!" He added this, as Cosima recorded in her diary, "in such a humorous tone we had to laugh heartily."[77]

That he who suffers injury has never far to look for ridicule is a bit of folk-wisdom whose validity Wagner experienced personally time and again. The onset of erysipelas, the deformity that invited both teasing and complacent tingles of horror, might strike at any time, with no premonitory warning as to when or why. In his autobiography, he surmised that "relapse of the erysipelas threatened in the wake of any inflammation,," and he offers as an example a merry

---

[74] Wagner, *Sämtliche Briefe*, v. V, p. 330.
[75] Cosima Wagner, *Diaries*, July 27, 1878.
[76] Glasenapp, v. I, p. 93.
[77] Cosima Wagner, *Diaries*, February 9, 1881.

evening gathering at the home of his friend Karl Ritter at which he was holding forth as usual, and had begun reading aloud E. T. A. Hoffmann's fairy-tale, *The Golden Pot*. Caught up in the excitement of the story, his listeners had neglected to add wood to the fire in stove, and no one noticed "that the room was gradually growing colder. Even before I had come to the end of my reading, to the horror of my audience, I sat once more with a swollen, red nose, and was forced to drag myself home to attend to the perennially intense assault of my malady."[78]

Scene 4

The Return of Kapellmeister Kreisler

Perhaps the subject of Wagner's reading *The Golden Pot* from E. T. A. Hoffmann's *Fantasy Pieces in the Manner of Callot* was not entirely without blame in his relapse, for the central character of the author's fairy-tale, all his life among his favorite pieces of literature, displayed manifest similarities to the speaker. In his heated fantasy, the hero, Anselmus, "condemned by fate to suffer misfortune and to communicate it wherever he might go,"[79] sees himself pursued by demons, and shrunk by a sorcerer down to a Tom Thumb. As Richard must have known, Hoffmann had completed this fantasy piece on the very New Year's Eve of 1813[80] on which he had met the highly cultured Adolf Wagner, Richard's uncle, in whom — to the astonishment of both — he recognized his inspiration for

---

[78] Wagner, *Mein Leben*, p. 545.
[79] Glasenapp, v. I, p. 118.
[80] Gregor-Dellin, p. 21.

The Golden Pot. The English book *The Miseries of Human Life*, which had given the writer the idea of the perennially unlucky fellow Anselmus, namely, had been translated into German by Adolf Wagner.

Wagner's uncle, who spent his whole life "surrounded by a great jumble of books," in a dark study, impressed his nephew with a "tall pointed felt cap," such as he had seen worn previously only by "Bajazzo, a company of high-wire artists."[81] Since Adolf himself displayed other Hoffmannesque qualities, from the author of *The Golden Pot* and his art Richard quickly developed a penchant for associating the demonic with the fantastical, the uncanny with the comical. Richard let himself be infected by the fever of this "mad genius," particularly since his late father, Friedrich (whom he had never known) had numbered among the circle of Hoffman's friends. Even in later years, Wagner recalled the nearly familial affinity he had all his life felt towards E. T. A. Hoffmann. When a friend of Hoffmann's remarked on his "great likeness" to Wagner, the composer affirmed, "there may well be some truth to this observation."[82]

As a fourteen-year-old, he reports in *Mein Leben*, he had received the inspiration from Hoffman, "which over the course of many years rose to a level of eccentric excitement and held sway over me by its so strange worldview,"[83] a view that still manifested itself in the eccentric impulses of the adult. The figure of Kapellmeister Johannes Kreisler from the realm of art exemplifies this form of existence, which bows to reality only insofar as it yields to the bizarre productions of

---

[81] Wagner, *Mein Leben*, p. 15.
[82] Glasenapp, v. VI, p. 130.
[83] Wagner, *Mein Leben*, p. 24.

fantasy. In the invention of this "mad genius" who became the archetype of the ecstatic artist, Hoffmann had created a literary alter-ego for himself; everything real life denied his creator, who earned his bread as a jurist in civil service, was allowed Kreisler. Hoffman depicted his Kapellmeister in a caricature as a wild dancer with a Mohawk hairdo and flying coat-tails, from whose long clay pipe those creative soap-bubbles rise, to which—as the conclusion of *The Golden Pot* reveals—the alcoholically inspired fairy-tale itself belongs.

Devoted, like his creator, to the art of composition, Kreisler lived with a tomcat capable of human speech by the name of Murr, whose *Life and Opinions of Tomcat Murr* is one of Hoffmann's best-known novels. Tomcat Murr's origins also lie in that world of magic, alongside whose higher plane of existence so-called reality pales—the reality in which Hoffmann had to carry out his dry clerical duties as Supreme Court Counsel. Filled with contempt for the prosaic quotidian, Kreisler devoted himself entirely to the conjuring of the "spirit realm of tones," in which the young Richard Wagner was his devoted follower. "Music was altogether just the demonic to me," his young admirer recalled, "a mystically sublime monstrous essence."[84] It bestowed on its creator the aura of the omnipotence of artistic inspiration—albeit in real life, the stigma of the amusing oddball.

---

[84] *Ibid.*, p. 39.

"*Atlas of Music.*" In 1877, *Puck* took aim at Wagner's private weakness for satin ("*Atlas*"), silk roses, and French notions.

"In fact," Hoffman says of his crazy Kapellmeister, "everything he did, above all his life in art, contrasted so starkly with anything you could call sensible and proper,"[85] that he presented himself—one might well complete the sentence—as a model to a fantasy-prone hot-head like Wagner, who on occasion would sign his

---

[85] E.T.A. Hoffmann, *Sämtliche poetischen Werke.* Hannsludwig Geiger, ed., (Wiesbaden, undated), v. I, *Phantasiestücke in Callots Manier*, p. 283.

letters: "Richel, the mad Kapellmeister."[86] His tendency towards extravagant dress was also adopted from Kreisler, whose predilection for a particular Chinese dressing gown may well have influenced the taste of the older Wagner such that he assembled a whole closetful of expensive dressing gowns of silk, satin, and damask in all the colors of the rainbow. The weekly humor magazine *Puck* accordingly dubbed the composer "Atlas of Music."[87]

Since even the young Wagner set great store by putting every idea into practice as soon as possible and thus realizing in actuality whatever played out in his head, the scholar went on the lookout for a Hoffmannesque character on the streets of Leipzig—and found him. As though obsessed by the fictional character "and other musical ghosts of my favorite author," he wrote in his memoir, "I thought it my good fortune finally to have discovered such a real-life original: this ideal musician, in whom for a time I harbored the fantastic idea of having discovered at least a second 'Kreisler,' was a certain Flachs. At all the garden concerts, the principal source of my musical education, I encountered this tall, exceptionally gaunt person with a particularly narrow head and a most peculiar way of walking, carrying himself, and speaking." While savoring the musical sounds, he was struck by the eccentric's "singular convulsive nodding of the head and sigh-like inflating of the cheeks," which Richard, under the influence of

---

[86] Wagner, *Sämtliche Briefe*, v. II, p 264. "Richel" was Wagner's family nickname.
[87] A pun on "Atlas," both the German and an archaic English word for satin.

his reading of Hoffmann, "interpreted as demonic ecstasy."[88]

For a time, according to Wagner, Flachs became his "most intimate friend; everywhere one saw the slight sixteen-year-old youth going around with the oddly wobbling bean-pole," and even in his Bayreuth days, Wagner recalled him with amusement, and "mimicked his friend Flachs," as Cosima noted, "graphically for the children."[89] Thanks to the good relations of the eccentric with the Leipzig musicians, he was even able to help the aspiring composer to a debut success. The pseudo-Kreisler orchestrated an aria composed by Wagner for wind band, which was presented at a garden concert in 1829 in Leipzig's Rosental Park.[90] Thus, to the sound of trumpets and kettle-drums, did Wagner set out on his journey to world renown.

He always carried the memory of E. T. A. Hoffmann, Kapellmeister Kreisler, and his doppelganger around in his valise. Anyone who knew Wagner in his altogether normal "mad high-spirits," in which, "often for hours on end," he would captivate a gathering "with sage and witty conversation," might recognize in him the reincarnation of that fantastical-demonic triad with all its accompanying Hoffmannesque manifestations. "To reinforce his expositions," reported Angelique am Rhyn, who had almost daily contact with Wagner during his Tribschen period, "sometimes with his hands, arms, or with his entire body, he carried out memorable, almost rhythmic motions, that often rose to the most daring leaps—to *'murksis,'* such as E. T. A.

---

[88] Wagner, *Mein Leben*, p. 39.
[89] Cosima Wagner, *Diaries*, December 20, 1879.
[90] Karl-Heinz Kröplin, *Richard Wagner. Eine Chronik*, (Leipzig, 1887), p. 29.

The Laughing Wagner

Hoffmann describes of his Kapellmeister Kreisler," — to which Wagner would add acrobatic tricks from his own repertoire. "He loved especially," his landlord's daughter continued, "to do gymnastics on the house façade, from one window to another, filling his guests with terror and amazement.."[91]

Terror and amazement, which sometimes resolved into the release of laughter, formed the curve of tension with which Wagner captured his audience in real life as in the theater, where instead of comical easing of tension, he injected melodramatic "transfiguration." Many found the inability to free themselves from Wagner's dramaturgical force as "demonic" in fact. His literary friend Malwida von Meysenbug saw him as a person, "quite ruled by his demon,"[92] in the good as well as the less agreeable sense.

Wagner's effervescent high spirits could turn at any moment to sharp-tongued and even wounding malice, which his century ascribed to the nature of the "demonic." Everyone who knew Wagner feared his "strangely demonic humor,"[93] which spared no one. Cosima herself noted the "remarkably demonic streak with which he, without the least intentional malice, deals with people." As she expressed it, when he "bares his barb," he "invariably and with demonic accuracy finds the soft spot."[94] Her spouse himself explained that this attribute concealed his instinctive disdain for hypocrisy and false piety. "My life-demon," Wagner said, "discards all artificial pretense,"[95] which

---

[91] Otto, p. 387.
[92] Barth/Mack/Voss, p. 361.
[93] Gregor-Dellin, p. 832.
[94] Cosima Wagner, *Diaries*, September 29, 1881.
[95] Glasenapp, v. IV, p. 30.

he described as "a powerful, grayish beast,"[96] as though he had actually encountered such a one. This monster emanating from his unconscious persecuted him with "most peculiar, virtually demonic misfortune," and "thwarted me at every step."[97]

From the Dutchman, tired unto death, to Siegfried, doomed to death, his heroes sang arias on this theme. For their creator, the demonic was from the beginning attuned with the musical, specifically that "demonic" that in its "monstrousness" transports people away from pale everyday reality, and not necessarily heavenwards. In actuality, it was the appalling which the composer-to-be first associated with the tones of sorcery: Weber's *Freischütz* filled the boy with the "thrill of terror and the fear of spirits."[98] Moreover, it inspired him to the production of "costumes and masks," whose "grotesque painting" he remembered in advanced age just as clearly as his home-made boar that ran on rollers.

For Wagner, inseparably associated with the electrifying music of *Freischütz*, which he memorialized in the *Nibelungen-Ring*, was its creator, who likewise displayed traits reminiscent of Hoffmann's characters: Carl Maria von Weber, whose "thoroughly tender, suffering, and spiritually transfigured aspect," inspired the student "with ecstatic empathy," even "spellbound" him with holy "dread." The court Kapellmeister caused a sensation among the Dresden citizens with his pet, a capuchin monkey named Schnuff Weber. In addition, according to Wagner, he drew attention by a "severely

---

[96] *Ibid.*, v. III, p. 428.
[97] *Ibid.*, v. III, p. 429.
[98] Wagner, *Mein Leben*, p. 18.

The Laughing Wagner

limping gait,"[99] on whose account those city-folk fond of mockery gave him the nick-name "Limping Mary."[100] Following his daily rehearsal, as the Kapellmeister limped past Richard's window, he thought he saw in him, at once disabled and sublime, a "super-human being," who absolutely inspired emulation.

A wet blanket was thrown on this enthusiasm when Wagner's mother introduced her son, nine years old at the time, to the famous composer. To Weber's friendly inquiry, "what I wanted to become, whether a musician perhaps, my mother said that though I was quite obsessed with *Freischütz*, she nonetheless saw nothing in me that bespoke musical talent. This," the memoirist commented dryly, "was most correctly observed by my mother."[101]

Nonetheless Richard did develop musical talent, even rising to succeed "Limping Mary" as Royal Saxon Kapellmeister, thanks to a circumstance related only indirectly to musical art: quartered in the tiny attic chamber of a Dresden "court silver cleaner's widow, who supplied him all day long with the well-known watery Saxon coffee as virtually [his] only nourishment,"[102] the fourteen-year-old devoted himself to crafting verses, such as he had encountered in the dramas of Shakespeare, Schiller, Kotzebue, as well as step-father Geyer.

The tragedy in the style of "Sturm und Drang," whose plot he devised himself, was called *Leubald* or also

---

[99] *Ibid.*, p. 35.
[100] Cosima Wagner, *Diaries*, December 25, 1880.
[101] Wagner, *Mein Leben*, p. 35.
[102] *Ibid.*, p. 27.

Leubald and Adelaide, the heroine's name derived from a well-known Beethoven song. The hero's "pregnant name!"[103] in turn, was meant to point to the heroic "Richard the Lionheart," as well as the "House of the Red and White Lions," in which the author of the tragedy had been born. Leubald's motto, "Weep Not — Only Slay, Only Slay!,"[104] revealed unmistakably that Richard's pleasure in risky overstepping of the bounds of convention had also put down stakes in his literary production.

Although this first drama by the young Richard, who still bore the name Geyer at the time, far exceeded *The Devil's Mill on Wienerberg* in the demonic, and Shakespeare's *Hamlet* in length, it was totally ineffectual. People were either unable or simply unwilling to comprehend it. He had delivered unto the world evidence of his undeniable artistry, and the world — in the persons of his family — gave him the cold shoulder. From his uncle Adolf, intimate of the gloomy E. T. A. Hoffmann who his nephew expected would give his thriller a sympathetic reading, the "voluminous manuscript" elicited icy astonishment, and from his family, downright "dismay."[105]

This may have been due to the fact that when it came to sadistic perversion, the young man had set himself no limits: blood gushes in great quantities, rape is enthusiastically indulged in, incest committed, everyone seems bent on slaughtering everyone else, and in the end most of the "42 people [who] in the course of the play" are massacred — in the words of the

---

[103] Richard Wagner, *Leubald*. Ein Trauerspiel, in: Programmheft VII der Bayreuther Festspiele, 1988, p. 150.
[104] *Leubald*, p. 106.
[105] Wagner, *Mein Leben*, p. 27

The Laughing Wagner

memoirist—"return as ghosts because I would otherwise have run out of characters in the last act."[106] An exaggeration, to be sure, but ultimately the whole play was one big exaggeration.

"The horror was great," Wagner wrote of the reaction of his family, all the more since in addition, the student as it turned out had dismally failed his school requirements, and was kept back. He was treated as though he had committed a "crime." Richard, the unacknowledged genius, had bet the house on a single throw, and had lost.

In this moment of abject failure, one redeeming thought occurred to him: something was still missing—something that would bring this masterpiece from the hand of a tender youth to life. "As people truly deafened me with their exclamations of woe over my lost time and my eccentric direction," he wrote in *Mein Leben*, "a wondrous inner comfort remained to me to offset the disaster that had befallen. I knew what no one else could know—namely that my work could truly be judged only when it had been furnished with the music I had determined to write myself."[107]

Though tinged with irony, this reminiscence, recorded more than forty years after the family's ostracism, was nonetheless no exaggeration, as is attested by Cosima in an 1870 diary entry. While the composer was at work on the *Ring*, she set down his comically exasperated exclamation: "'Oh! I am no composer,' he says, 'I wanted to learn just enough to compose *Leubald und*

---

[106] *Ibid.*, p. 28.
[107] *Ibid.*, p. 34.

Adelaide; and so it has remained, only the subjects have changed.'"[108]

But under what "subject" was this adolescent extra-curricular work, which drove Richard into the art of music, to be catalogued? Since the play was not, as uncle Adolf had already adjudged it, to be considered an artistic entity, the question becomes whether it represents an example of a horror play to test the endurance of an audience held hostage, or, on the other hand, a piece of literary high comedy, scarcely a line of which fails to evoke inane laughter. In retrospect, Wagner seems to have preferred the latter.

Nonetheless, the fiasco, as he affirms in *Mein Leben*, was not entirely without effect. At an early trial reading, its demonic dimension at least proved effective. After his sister Ottilie had several times submitted "affectionately [to] the torments" of his "mysterious, albeit not unemotional reading," she was treated by the author to a recitation of "one of the most hair-raising scenes," in which several of the Ten Commandments were violated at once. What happened next was textbook: in the midst of the reading, "a violent storm broke out; a bolt of lightning struck very near us, the thunder roared, and my sister thought she must plead with me to halt the reading. She soon realized the impossibility of moving me to that end, and bore it with touching devotion."[109]

How grandiose and simultaneously shattering must the music have sounded in Richard's inner ear: all the mass murders and rapes, as well as Adelaide's vampirism—"thus will I suck at your wound and gulp

---

[108] Cosima Wagner, *Diaries*, January 31, 1870.
[109] Wagner, *Mein Leben*, p. 31.

down life with your blood!"[110] — set to audacious melodies! Unfortunately, these were never to be written, because, as their author adds laconically in *Mein Leben*, the manuscript was "unfortunately lost."

No doubt for the same reason the actual scope of his *Leubald* vision remained hidden from his sisters, who spread the following concerning the work among the family circle: "At one demonic point, there is supposedly a live person who walks up to a ghost, who, however, warns him off in a muffled, cadaverous voice, 'Back, touch me not, for my nose crumbles to dust if it is touched!'"[111] This was of course a malicious fabrication with which the teasers — as at the time of "Already I hear the knight trotting!" — were trampling his artist's pride.

What did they even know of the magnificent curse aria Leubald flings at a world he despises?

> *"Cursed heart, why do you beat against my breast,*
> *It is cursed! Accursed word, why do you fly*
> *From the cursed mouth! — Accursed hand,*
> *Why do you strike at your most cursed brain!*
> *What are you thinking, brain, what cursed thoughts!*
> *O, I will curse, yes, I can curse!*
> *I will curse the creation, and nature!*
> *The world, that lascivious whore will I curse,*
> *Humans I curse; they are accursed all alike!*
> *O could I but curse insanity into my brain!*
> *The world is insanity, and I am mad!"*[112]

---

[110] *Leubald*, p. 144.
[111] Kloss, p. 29.
[112] *Leubald*, p. 182.

No, his all too prosaic sisters had no idea that hidden in the figure of Leubald lay the highly expressive ego of their little brother, nor could they appreciate the epigrammatic pith with which Adelaide, just before being strangled by her lover, had pointedly epitomized the peculiar nature of their relation:

"*O Leubald, weak am I, and you quite mad!*"[113]

Does this diagnosis, at least in the comic-demonic sense that E. T. A. Hoffmann bestowed on the word, not fit the poet of *Leubald*? At all events, even at the time of his celebrity as composer of *Rienzi*, the *Allgemeine Wiener Musikzeitung* found fit to remind Wagner's bevy of devotees that their star of the hour, now dressed in silver-trimmed tails at the podium of the Dresden Court Orchestra, had "once" been considered "a kind of mad genius."[114]

---

[113] *Leubald*, p. 196.
[114] Helmut Kirchmeyer, *Das zeitgenössische Wagner-Bild*, v. II, 1842-1845, (Regensburg, 1967), p. 74.

Act II

A Dog's Life

*"The most ridiculous mirth
Often comes over me in the same hour
As the most murderous melancholy."*[115]

Scene 1

The Tympani Fiasco

The failure of the *Leubald* project was not enough to dampen Richard's ambitious plans for the future. But though he remained true to his vision of the laurel-wreathed genius soaring above the common mass of humanity, his "demon of ill luck" remained true to him as well. Each fresh attempt to dazzle his contemporaries with an art work of high originality was foiled by his enemies' malice. And though "in ecstatic dreams"[116] he once again imagined himself eye to eye with Beethoven and Shakespeare, he nonetheless "woke up in tears," because this "picture of most sublime, transcendent originality" was forced to yield to the grim-grey reality of everyday life. His whole youthful life as he remembered it consisted of an emotional roller-coaster, on which he saw himself, like some figure in a tale of Hoffmann, by turns soaring genius and slain hero, object of cult-like worship and victim of dismissive indifference.

---

[115] Wagner, *Sämtliche Briefe*, v. VI, p. 56
[116] Wagner, Mein Leben, p. 37.

When it came to emotional roller-coasters, gymnastic feats, and erysipelas, his youthful life lasted well into the Bayreuth years. Even in his sixties, when he had finally achieved lasting international fame, he chose not to abandon the pleasures of being as unconventional and unseasonable as he had been as a child. When the first festivals concluded in both enormous triumph for his ideas and enormous deficits for his purse, he noted "that no artist had ever been so honored,"[117] following that with a despairing "never again, never again."[118]

After every imaginable honor, good luck wishes from Kaiser Wilhelm I, homage paid him several times by the Grand Duke of Weimar (descendant of that Prince Konstantin who had very nearly been his ancestor), the Master was honored at a banquet to celebrate the closing of the first *Ring* cycle where he was proclaimed the new Siegfried. The tributes of all sorts, the wild applause and endless salutes were recorded in Cosima's diary: it had been a "very, very lovely evening."[119]

On Wagner's reaction, she was silent, and with good reason. For once again, the Master, in response to the incessant flattery, had allowed himself the indulgence of a Till Eulenspiegel-like self-parody. "Adorned with a silver laurel-crown a female admirer had bestowed on him," noted a supporter, "he strutted through the rows of guests, showing us the 'genius as child.'"[120] His actual attitude toward such head-adornment had struck Lilli Lehmann years earlier, when he presented her with

---

[117] Gregor-Dellin, p. 716 (Rückblick auf die Bühnenfestspiele, 1876).
[118] Gregor-Dellin, p. 724.
[119] Cosima Wagner, *Diaries*, August 18, 1876.
[120] Ludwig Schemann, Meine *Erinnerungen an Richard Wagner*, (Stuttgart, 1902), p. 15.

a "large silver laurel wreath, on whose leaves his complete works had been engraved. But I believe I recall," the singer wrote, "that he mocked the wreath."[121]

"Adorned with a laurel wreath." The pose as Caesar in which in 1865 the Munich *Punch* caricatured him is said to have moved even him to laughter.

Wagner's laurel-wreath pantomime at the festival banquet, which his supporters interpreted as the expression of "innocent high-spirited joy," must have reflected the satirical frame of mind of the object of so much adulation: though his childhood dream of being surrounded by devoted disciples may finally have come

---
[121] Otto, p. 528.

true, nevertheless the ridiculous silver wreath smacked of the sentiment that his elevation to cult object belonged not to the seriousness of art, but rather to the jokes of a comedy routine. At the sight of a picture of Goethe with a laurel-wreath once, Wagner had remarked that it looked "as though he is waiting to be served."[122]

Among the contemporaries hoping to borrow a leaf from the composer's laurel-wreath was the Munich costume-maker whose bear-skin cloaks, steer-horn helmets, and tin Valkyrie corsages contribute to the amusement of Wagner critics to this day. When he complained to the Master of Bayreuth how unrecognized he still was despite his artistic accomplishments, Wagner replied with feigned earnestness, "You expect to be famous in Germany after a mere fifty-one years? No, my friend, at least sixty years. Look at me, at how long I've been working at this thing—how bloody little I've achieved!"

"Honored Master," replied the Germanic outfitter, whom Wagner's irony had eluded, "permit me to point out however that, if on every concert program one's name appears three or four times, then I believe one might flatter oneself to have achieved a great deal already!" As though in agreement, at that moment a band in the park began to play the prelude to *Lohengrin*. Doepler, who promptly saw himself vindicated, grinned at Wagner.

---

[122] Cosima Wagner, *Diaries*, November 23, 1879.

"Well, yes, yes," Wagner replied, stamping his foot in mock anger. "But how, *how* they are playing it! Terrible! One would just like to escape somewhere!"[123]

That precisely the most sublime masterworks should be the source of displeasure for their creator was among Wagner's earliest and most painful experience—first, because the divine fire of inspiration is rarely communicable to a work's performers, who often find themselves set unsolvable technical problems of interpretation; and second, because only rarely does the public prove equal to the extreme demands of the highest levels of artistic achievement, applying instead standards suitable to artistic mediocrity at best.

But since Wagner nonetheless did set his performers the highest demands because he felt called to the highest levels of achievement, he was beside himself with annoyance when the reception of his work failed to match his ambitions—even though he had actually expected no different outcome. "It has often proven true," he said, half in jest, "that the womb of German motherhood is capable of conceiving the loftiest geniuses in the world; whether the organs of reception of the German folk can prove worthy of the noble births of these chosen mothers still remains to be seen."[124]

The first creative work came from his pen in the year 1825, when he was a student in secondary school, and his already ripening poetic ambitions were challenged by an assignment that must have seemed charming to a twelve-year-old rhymester. As Wagner recalls in *Mein Leben*, a fellow student by the name of Starke had died suddenly, and the funeral, to be occasioned by great

---

[123] Otto, p. 528.

[124] C. F. Glasenapp, *Wagner-Encyklopädie*, (Leipzig, 1891), v. I, p. 357.

pomp and circumstance was to be "elevated" by the reading of a poem in celebration of the departed. The poem was then to be printed. The thought of being first acclaimed and then printed gave wings to Richard's creation of a precocious masterwork of poetic art.

Unfortunately, recognition was not forthcoming, because the originality of Richard's offering was thrown into question. As Wagner explained in retrospect, the teacher had detected "a certain descriptive pomposity far exceeding the imaginative capacity of a boy my age." Among other things, in order to memorialize the departed with appropriate dignity, the fledgling poet had taken as his model a work by the Englishman Joseph Addison, not widely known in Leipzig.

In his tragedy *Cato*, which culminates with that Roman Stoic's suicide (and contains the germ of Patrick Henry's "give me liberty or give me death"), Richard had discovered a philosophically profound monologue that seemed to him to touch on the inherently tragic death of his fellow student. To the gymnasiast's ill fortune, his source, an English grammar text, was known among the faculty, so that his adaptation fell under suspicion of plagiary. Worse still, the words appropriated from Addison, "The stars shall fade away, the sun himself/Grow dim with age," provoked in his teacher an "all but insulting smile."[125] Presumably, the teacher had been amused also by the following lines, inspired by the Englishman, a century dead, which proclaimed, "Unhurt amid the war of elements,/The wrecks of matter, and the crush of worlds!" the soul of

---

[125] Wagner, *Mein Leben*, p. 21.

fellow student Starke was destined to "flourish in immortal youth."

The blow struck home; Wagner suffered indescribably over the shipwreck of his illusions. Yet, this would not be the last word of fate. If nearly every artistic achievement proved the source of perennial frustration for Wagner, nearly every defeat was transformed after the fact into a splendid triumph. The stimulus provided by *Cato*, which had borne no fruit at Starke's funeral, came once more to the fore in *The Flying Dutchman*. The death-smitten Roman's exclamation returns here in the song of the seafarer, longing just as fervently for death, and summoning his whole capacity for suffering to call into the void, "When will the annihilating blow ring out that shall crush the world?!"

Mystically attracted to tragic themes, the youth threw himself into composition of a tragedy in the style of Sophocles about the "death of Odysseus," though he foundered on the all too ambitious endeavor. To hone his poetical skills he studied ancient Greek with a tutor so he could read Sophocles in the original, whose works he already knew in uncle Adolf's translation, and to profit from the ancient master on future projects.

Unfortunately, his plans collapsed comically this time too, stymying his acquisition of the language of classical drama: as it happened, the living room of the rather inept teacher opened "onto a tannery, whose repulsive odor afflicted my nerves so that it thoroughly spoiled Sophocles and all things Greek for me."[126] In the long term, though, he did not let this deter him, and twenty years later — an echo of his ill-fated "Odysseus" — created a no less tragic, equally peripatetic hero. In

---

[126] *Ibid.*, p. 46.

1848, with "The Death of Siegfried,' Wagner laid the cornerstone of his grand Bayreuth project about *The Ring of the Nibelung*.

Its dramatic score, which counts for Wagnerians among the "Seven Wonders of the World" (the other six are *The Flying Dutchman, Tannhäuser, Lohengrin, Tristan, Meistersinger,* and *Parsifal*), also had its modest, halting, and—if we are to believe his reports—even decidedly comic beginnings in his school days. Since Richard's family was not to know that his proscribed drama *Leubald and Adelaide* had begun sprouting musical blossoms, the fifteen-year-old contrived to acquire the foundation of composition in secret, which manifested itself immediately in the form of sonatas, quartets, an aria (orchestrated, as we know, for wind band by Flachs) and a "pastoral opera" doubtless inspired by Carl Maria von Weber.

The youth hoped for his first professional appraisal from the Magdeburg Music Director Kienlen, to whom he was introduced by his sister Clara, now an opera singer. This musician, too, (whom Wagner recalled as "Herr Kühnlein") displayed conspicuous Hoffmanesque qualities, not the least of them Mozart worship. Kienlen's devotion was, however, coupled with a no less "passionate denigration of Weber" that assumed pathological proportions. According to Wagner, this "aging, sickly, and unfortunately also alcoholic" artist read "only one book: Goethe's *Faust*, and in this volume there was not a page lacking a passage marked with either an ecstatic interpretation pertaining to Mozart or a demeaning reference to Weber." After the Director had ridden this hobby-horse at length, the turn of the youthful composer came round. Clara's husband, Heinrich Wolfram, had presented the collected works of his hopeful brother-in-law, and finally, according to Wagner, had ventured to inquire "what he had found in my works. 'Not a note that's good,' came his serene reply."[127]

When Richard's passion for music, along with the weaknesses in his command of it came to light, his mother was moved to arrange violin lessons for him with a Leipzig violinist by the name of Sipp. Wagner recalled later that he had "tortured my mother and sisters terribly for three months [with the instrument] from my wonderful little room,"[128] which led to a waning of their enthusiasm, and then in turn his own. From then on, he distanced himself from the violin, perhaps because in truth he possessed no talent for this instrument. "He had a quick intelligence, but he was lazy and refused to practice," Sipp recalled sixty years later, adding, "he was my worst student."[129]

To be fair, it should be noted that Richard never nurtured the ambition to become a virtuoso. All his life he avoided the violin, and played piano, by his own estimation, as "a rat, the flute." Wagner's ambition was to compose like Beethoven and conduct like Weber — he asked no more. His musical education pursued an erratic course, dictated more by chance than by any well-defined system, even if with autodidactic diligence he studied J. B. Logier's renowned method of composition, borrowed from the loan-library of Clara Schumann's father, Friedrich Wieck (without, be it said, ever paying the accrued fees). Following a crash course in harmony theory from a Gewandhaus musician named Müller, the young Wagner was

---

[127] *Ibid.*, p. 41.
[128] *Ibid.*, p. 43.
[129] Kröplin, p. 31.

initiated by the Leipzig musical pedagogue Theodor Weinlig into the mysteries of the art of counterpoint, whose "rigorous style" reappears in late homage to the Cantor of the Thomaskirche in the third act of *Meistersinger*.

In 1830, the same year the *studiosus musicus* left Sipp's tutelage (or was dismissed by him), he presented to the people of Leipzig a sort of "Surprise Symphony," derived not from Haydn, but inspired rather by Beethoven's Ninth. Wagner had composed it himself, in B major, and had won the highly regarded conductor Heinrich Dorn for a Christmas Eve performance. Though Dorn joked later that "already at the rehearsal the orchestra split its sides laughing,"[130] he bore some of the blame himself.

Haydn's notation to his most famous symphony: "It was important to me to surprise the audience with something new, and to open in a brilliant manner," might well have come from the seventeen-year-old Wagner. To become famous with a single stroke, that was the thing! The circumstances of this "single stroke," however, were as follows: "The main theme of the allegro was of a four-measure nature," explained the composer. "After every fourth measure, though, a fifth measure completely unconnected with the melody was interpolated, marked by a particular tympani stroke on the second beat of the measure. Since this stroke was rather exposed," as he observed even at the first rehearsal, "the timpanist, who constantly thought he was making a mistake, turned timid and failed to give the beat the proper emphasis called for in the score. To my genuine uneasiness, however, Dorn

---

[130] Barth/Mack/Voss, p. 292.

singled out the embarrassed timpanist and insisted he play it with the emphasis indicated in the score." Informed later of Dorn's "delight in mockery," Wagner would learn, unfortunately too late, that the conductor "on this occasion was making a joke,"[131] at the debutant's expense, of course.

The man with the Kettle Drum. Even if Wagner's first attempts "to achieve fame with a single stroke" foundered, he soon became, as here in the humor magazines, a master of self-promotion

---

[131] Wagner, *Mein Leben*, p. 59.

Dorn's stock went up; the people of Leipzig had their Christmas joke, for in addition to the tympani stroke, which was sounded with clockwork precision, Wagner deployed the various sections of the orchestra against one another as though it were a pitched battle among Hoffmannesque ghost armies. So that this "mystical" conflict might strike the eye of the conductor already on perusal of the score, the young artist planned to write out the parts of the brass in black ink, strings in red, and woodwinds in green, though the latter turned out to be impossible because green ink was not to found in Leipzig.

On Christmas Eve, whose high-point traditionally is the exchange of gifts, the anticipation of the citizens of Leipzig was already quite great. The festively adorned theater filled, but then the Christmas spirit of the audience quickly gave way to a certain unease when the motif of the "black" brass instruments sounded, evoking a mood more appropriate to Good Friday. Faces grew even longer when the aggressive allegro of the "red" strings followed, met in turn with clockwork precision by the dreadful tympani stroke from the "black" world, which the responsible musician produced "with malicious brutality." The audience understood they were being presented eccentric stuff, falling well beyond the bounds of the seasonally as well as the musically palatable. "From initial astonishment at the relentlessness of the timpanist," as biographer Glasenapp renders the scene, "the audience transitioned to undisguised annoyance, then finally over into merriment deeply distressing to the composer."[132]

Seated in the parterre, the aspiring composer was witness to the snickering curiosity his repetitive fortissimo timpani stroke evoked: "I heard my neighbors," he wrote, "calculating and signaling this recurrence in advance. What I suffered under this, cognizant of the accuracy of their calculations, is indescribable. I lost consciousness. Finally, I awoke as the overture, to which I had scorned affixing any of the conventionally banal ending formulas, broke off quite unexpectedly, as though from a baffling dream. All the impressions of a Hoffmannesque fantasia paled beside the strange condition in which I came to myself."

At the conclusion of the piece, general perplexity reigned. The audience seemed incapable of so much as demonstrating displeasure; not even "proper laughter" made itself heard—only, as Wagner recalled it, "the greatest general astonishment over so unusual an event."[133] No one "knew what to make of it," wrote the malicious Dorn, "when the players, after a long, confusing musical scrum, suddenly put away their instruments, their work being done."[134]

In his memoirs, Wagner dwelt to the full on every last detail of the traumatic experience. "But nothing," he wrote describing the ensuing moments, "could compare to the agony I now suffered having to face the porter once more. The peculiar look he gave me left an indelible impression on me, and for a long time I stayed away from the parterre of the Leipzig Theater."

---

[132] Glasenapp, v. I, p. 133.
[133] Wagner, *Mein Leben*, p. 60.
[134] Glasenapp, v. I, p. 133.

Not the theater *per se*, however. That here and nowhere else his laurels would thrive, namely, was beyond question for him. Compared to everyday life, it offered the infinitely more attractive alternative, promising this protagonist the merited applause his normal existence withheld. Only in the theater were achievement and reward connected in an immediate causal relation. But of course the opposite was also true: consequences followed hard on the heels of a botched performance.

Thanks to Wagner's distinctive humor, his memoirs read like an endless string of failures, bad luck, and embarrassments. His intentionally byzantine, yet always witty descriptions make clear that we are dealing not at all with the pompous, narcissistic posturer caricatures made of him from the outset, but rather with a man of genius as articulate as he was intelligent who, like Hoffmann and Heine, particularly enjoyed satirizing himself.

A perfect example of such humor at his own expense is provided by a memorable concert he produced in Magdeburg, on May 2, 1835, only a few years after the Leipzig tympani fiasco. At his slender 22 years he had already risen to local fame, and his E. T. A. Hoffmann inspired opera *The Fairies* demonstrated that he had mastered the composer's creative idiom no less than the conductor's interpretive one. As Music Director of Magdeburg, he thought back with satisfaction of his predecessor, the alcoholic Mozartian, Kienlen, who had once criticized him so utterly.

Unhappily, already at that time Wagner excelled in the art of turning big-hearted friends into hard-hearted creditors. Because his theater salary was entirely inadequate for him both to repay his enormous debts and support his spend-thrift lifestyle, he dreamed up a lucrative event with audience appeal, at which besides his own works, and Beethoven's *Wellington's Victory*, on the program also were to be vocal offerings by Wilhelmine Schröder-Devrient, at that time the object of cult-like adoration. For the day following this concert that was certain to prove an unqualified triumph, he had invited his creditors in order to clean the slate once and for all.

The disaster began with the incredulity of the citizens of Magdeburg, who could not believe that Schröder-Devrient, glittering star of the opera firmament, would come to their city on the Elbe simply on account of the little Music Director—which indicated conversely that the stock of his credibility stood no higher than belief in his ability to pay his debts. The public apparently had no very great faith in his program selections, and the inflated price of admission contributed no doubt additionally to the "sparseness of the audience" in the hall of the inn "City of London." This occasioned a double "embarrassment" for the impresario: aside from his own disappointment, he had to cope with the displeasure of the Prima Donna, who was accustomed to packed houses (and who, by the way, not least because of her imposing physical presence, became the model of all Wagner's heroines, including his jubilant Valkyries). Nonetheless, on this occasion the Diva delivered Beethoven's song "Adelaide" (which had once inspired Wagner to compose *Leubald*), and she did so "ravishingly beautifully."

Then the notably elegant conductor—he "attempted to guard against the blunder of conducting with both hands by always pressing one arm akimbo against his side"[135] — performed a piece of his own composition, the overture to *Columbus*, a drama by his friend Theodor Apel, a largely unknown occasional poet, for whose patronage he owed the favor. Many in the Magdeburg audience already knew the Apel piece, and had not forgotten that despite expensive sets, "a plethora of splendid costumes," and Wagnerian incidental music, it had been more or less a flop.

So now Wagner tried showcasing his music on its own. Following the lines of the content of *Columbus*, the overture, "in not very arduously selected figurations," as the composer reported critically of himself, describes "the sea and if you will the ship on it too: only a powerful, passionately yearning and aspiring motif was discernable in the surge of the scene. This ensemble was now repeatedly and abruptly interrupted by an exotic motif appearing high in the violins at an extreme pianissimo, a diminuendoing whir, as though a Fata Morgana. I had commissioned three pairs of trumpets in various tunings for this purpose in order to perform this splendid and seductive dying motif with the most tender coloration and the most varied inflections: this was the promised land for which the hero's searching eye was scanning."[136]

Unfortunately, the Magdeburg audience apparently failed to grasp this intention, and was far more distracted by the shattering blast of trumpets, which, in the miserable acoustics of the inn's hall, created an "unbearably noisy effect," initiating the debacle that befell the young man both artistically and financially. "my 'Columbus Overture,' with its six trumpets, had already inspired all the listeners with terror, but now as

---

[135] *Ibid.*, v. I, p. 274.
[136] Wagner, *Mein Leben*, p. 60.

a finale came "Wellington's Victory" by Beethoven, which, in enthusiastic expectation of vast emoluments from unheard of receipts, I had outfitted with every imaginable orchestral extravagance. With costly, specially constructed machines, rifle and artillery fire on both French and English sides were recreated with great fidelity; drums and bugles doubled and tripled."

Thanks to the realism of the noise contrivances deployed, the conductor unleashed "a battle, more gruesome than was ever fought in a concert hall, as the orchestra assaulted the small auditorium with such overwhelming superiority that the audience finally gave up all resistance and literally beat a retreat." When, finally, the star of the evening herself, the great Wilhelmine, made a bee-line for the exit, "almost wringing her hands," this, as Wagner stressed, was "a token of a truly panic-stricken terror. Everyone dashed out, and ultimately the celebration of Wellington's victory turned into a pitiful effusion between me and the orchestra all alone."[137]

He was not long alone. For in the corridor in front of his lodging room, meanwhile, "a long double-row of ladies and gentlemen" had taken up positions, not as fans in quest of an autograph, but as creditors demanding their money. Thanks to the aid of a "trustworthy Jewess" by the name of Madame Gottschalk and an imaginative reference to his "wealthy acquaintances" in Leipzig, he succeeded in placating the angry ladies and gentlemen, and, as the debtor wittily put it, "making the hall outside my room passable again."

---

[137] *Ibid.*, p. 107.

Shortly afterwards, in March, 1836, Wagner's next magnum opus, *Das Liebesverbot*, was to do credit to the genre of "Grand Comic Opera." Intended once more for Magdeburg, and once more to be mounted in a special production from whose copious receipts Wagner hoped to wipe out his debts, this ambitious work with its "numerous and powerful ensemble numbers" in the event met with a failure overshadowing even that of the concert at the inn: it never took place.

Already the premiere, which would be its sole performance, stood under an unlucky star. All the singers suffered from faulty memories, which led to a "debilitating awkwardness." First and foremost, the tenor Freimüller, who was in any case "endowed with the weakest memory," attempted to manage his obvious deficiencies by acting that was characterized by southern ebullience; mostly, though, "with an immoderately thick and waving colored plume of feathers," all of which failed utterly, however, leaving the audience "completely in the dark" about the events on stage.[138]

The second attempt to perform *Das Liebesverbot* was intended not only to assure the success of the piece, but also to solve Wagner's past and current pressing financial problems. Since this would be the final production of the season, he had optimistically set the price of admission as high as possible, with the result that only "a few people" were in the theater, among them his advocate Madame Gottschalk, who together with her husband and a "Polish Jew in full costume" had taken seats in the orchestra.

---

[138] *Ibid.*, p. 122.

So only a few were granted the pleasure of experiencing a truly theatrical scene that fit the title of the piece admirably, without actually being a part of it. Two of the principal performers in *Das Liebesverbot*, namely, the leading soprano, Mrs. Pollert, and the second tenor, Mr. Schreiber, had chosen to ignore Mr. Pollert's "prohibition of love,"[139] initiating an adulterous affair he could no longer countenance. What Wagner had regarded as his last chance at obliterating his debts offered the jealous spouse a last chance at settling scores with his speedily exiting rival.

Even before the conductor could take up his baton, the cuckolded husband sneaked onto the set "to take vengeance on his wife's lover." Blind with rage, he sprang on the second tenor, beating him so soundly "that the unfortunate, blood streaming down his face, was forced to retire to the dressing room," in the passage way to which the prima donna "threw herself in desperation at her raging husband." The raving spouse, who shrank at nothing now, administered to her forthwith "blows of such force that she collapsed in convulsions."

The dramatic scene nearly led to a "general melee," for now other performers saw it as an opportunity to settle their own mutual scores. But the tumultuous evening did come to an abrupt end when the director called the gamecocks to order and, stepping in front of the curtain, announced the cancellation of the performance on account of "unforeseen obstacles." Wagner was forced to the depressing conclusion that herewith, "the end of my promising conducting and composing career

---

[139] "Das Liebesverbot" means "the prohibition of love" in German.

in Magdeburg, taken up with rather significant sacrifice," had arrived.[140]

Scene 2

In the Realm of the Fairy Amorosa

Simultaneous with the tragicomic setbacks he would forever associate with the name Magdeburg, his career as husband commenced, which would prove less comic than tragic. He was introduced to "the seriousness of life," as he outlined his first great love experience, in Bad Lauchstädt, where the Magdeburg Theater, whose Music Directorship he had applied for, made guest appearances in the summers. He encountered this still unfamiliar "seriousness of life" in the person of an actress whose name was Minna (formally, Wilhelmine), and was publicized in the theater company as "leading lady"—such an omen! [141]

Wagner's description of her troupe given in *Mein Leben* offers a vivid picture of what in his century was meant by "bohemian relationships." Having arrived at the resort village, the aspirant inquired after the residence of Theater Director Bethmann, to which finally an unwashed urchin promised to lead him. The boy was discovered to be the Director's offspring. And by chance, at that moment his "Papa" was making his way towards them down the street in nightshirt and sleeping cap. He broke out promptly in lament over some evil that had befallen him. By way of speedy

---

[140] *Ibid.*, p. 128.
[141] "*Erste Liebhaberin*," a double-entendre: the German theatrical term literally means "first lover."

remedy, and with measured ostentation, he pressed a silver coin into the hand of his young son, instructing him to procure him a shot from the nearest bar.

The young artist grasped at once the ambiguous nature of his future employer. Although the former protégé of the King of Prussia (who had once shown a keen interest in Bethmann's wife) displayed in word and manner the saccharine formality of a bygone era, it was nonetheless unmistakable that he had, through "incessant work running of the theater already gone profoundly downhill," and that "everything he did and surrounded himself with evidenced the most undignified deterioration." The new arrival found the wife of the director, lame in one foot, resting on a divan, while her lover, whose excessive devotion Bethmann often lamented, calmly smoked his pipe at her side.

Wagner soon also met his future colleague, the director Schmale, who was just then consulting with the theater manager, a "toothless old skin-and-bones," over which opera should be mounted next. At regular intervals he reached through the open window for a cherry branch, from which as calm as you please he plucked cherries, whose pits he spit noisily back out into the great outdoors. Wagner, who had in any case "a congenital distaste for fruit," decided to beat a hasty retreat.[142]

Now, as though directed from on high, Minna Planer made her entrance. Amid the general "dust-cloud of irresponsibility and meanness" reigning in Bethmann's chaotic troupe, the actress—nearly four years his senior, though she claimed to be younger—seemed to him a veritable fairy. Among all the "caricatures and masks" that populated the Bad Lauchstädt Wooden Theater,

---

[142] *Ibid.*, p. 94.

this magical being stood out for her total "absence of all theatrical pretension and comedic affectation." Small wonder that this daughter of a retired regimental bugler seemed to the future Music Director like a dream maiden out of a fairy tale. Fatefully, she soon thereafter assumed the role of the charming Fairy Amorosa, patron saint of love in Nestroy's magic farce, *The Evil Spirit Lumpazivagabundus*. Wagner decided to stay, and then and there he rehearsed the piece with her.

His idealization of the charming Minna-Amorosa was intensified by two incidents, through which she became acquainted with his personal idiosyncrasies. First was his passion for acrobatics, which Wagner had no intention of abandoning even as Municipal Music Director. Second was his regularly "blossoming" erysipelas, which compelled him to shun the public and keep to his bed.

Follow your Nose. Wagner's prominent organ, prone to swelling with erysipelas, offered caricaturists a welcome target—here in the Vienna *Floh*, with an odor of anti-Semitism.

Minna encountered Wagner the acrobat one night when, returning home late and having lost the key to his ground-floor apartment, he tried to gain entry through his window. Awakened by the noise, Minna, who lived above him, looked from her window into the darkness below and saw the new tenant balanced on his window sill. He took advantage of the opportunity of wishing her a good-night with a handshake, which—as he had calculated—forced his well-endowed neighbor "by bending her upper body far downwards" to offer him (beside the handshake) also a revealing view deep into her nightdress.[143] The two-person balancing act was successful, and Wagner was lost.

He met with even greater lack of inhibition on Minna's part when, "afflicted by erysipelas, from which I often suffered, and with a swollen, horribly distorted face I hid in my melancholy chamber away from all the world." To his surprise, Fairy Amorosa not only rose above the restriction bourgeois moral code placed on visits by ladies to gentlemen's rooms, but visited him repeatedly, indeed in the role of empathetic Samaritan. Since, as she assured him, "his distorted face was of absolutely no consequence" to her, she had no problem in pressing a kiss on the "rash, which I myself found so unpleasant I should ask her pardon for showing myself with it." She did so, indeed, "with a friendly calm and composure that had something almost of the motherly about it, in no way suggestive of callousness or want of feeling."[144]

Soon enough the besotted musician would learn this interpretation was premature. His were not the only bachelor's quarters the good fairy visited. For Minna

---

[143] *Ibid.*, p. 98.
[144] *Ibid.*, p. 98.

took a pragmatic view of love, honoring a practice, nearly de rigueur among actresses and dancers of the time: because theatrical remuneration hardly sufficed to support the lavish lifestyle of the artists, they let themselves be kept by well-to-do aficionados, and returned their kindness with favor that reserved to itself the freedom to switch beneficiary at will. When Wagner caught on to this practice and fell into paroxysms of jealousy, he had a taste of Fairy Amorosa's claws. Called to task, Minna made it clear she had no intention of dismissing her remunerative lovers, and Richard fell victim to the very rage he had so condescended to in Mr. Pollert.

That Minna had come from a humble background and may well have made her career by way of the casting couch had simply escaped him. Emma Herwegh, who had mocked Wagner as a "pocket edition of a man," called Minna a "good and true proletarian soul,"[145] which from the mouth of an 1848 revolutionary was not at all meant disparagingly. It was also on point. Compared to the effusive, true genius, who could count a Prince among his ancestors and whose uncle was a friend of E. T. A. Hoffmann, Minna was a thoroughly conventional soul without intellectual pretensions, for which she compensated with extravagant expectations with respect to her lifestyle.

More important to her than any short-lived fame were apparently stable finances at a high level, which seemed assured with the Music Director's income of her intended. Later too she insisted that all her husband's ventures be based on contractually fixed salaries, so she might be guaranteed a household with staff and

---

[145] Kapp, p. 111.

commensurate social standing. It was not least this frankly prosaic attitude that alienated Wagner from his heart's fairy, and time and again provoked ironic commentary. Thus, at the time of the 1849 insurrection in Dresden, he saw no other way of making his revolutionary activities palatable to the mistrustful Minna than "under the color of a permanent position" with a steady salary, which as future "Secretary of the Provisional Government" would accrue to him. "I had to put this to her," he confessed later, "and pretend something to myself."[146]

Since Richard loved Minna to the point of self-surrender, but at the same time refused to stop piling up new mountains of debt, she treated him — though he considered himself the chosen one — as just one among many. Annoyed by his jealous tantrums, from time to time she packed her bags and escaped into the blue with some solvent gallant from the worlds of petty nobility or business, pursued by her fiancé who had dreams of glory of dispatching his rival with whip and pistol. Nothing of the sort occurred, and far from ruining their relationship, Minna's constant episodes of faithlessness led instead to its becoming permanent. They quarreled relentlessly . . . oh, and by the way, decided to marry.

For a long time the fear of Minna's unpredictable dalliances would not leave him, and time and again he asked his fate, "why it had been my lot, at so young an age to encounter such a terrible, as it seemed to me life-poisoning experience."[147] Even in the midst of the marriage ceremony, the young groom was reminded of the bridal escapades. For the minister alluded in his

---

[146] Cosima Wagner, *Diaries*, December 13, 1878.
[147] Wagner, *Mein Leben*, p. 151.

sermon to a "friend unknown to me," who in their "time of trouble" would stand by their side. When Wagner, suspicious over what struck him as a salacious allusion, and looked the minister straight in the eye, the man of God quickly clarified "that this friend unknown to him . . . was Jesus."[148]

A good fourteen years later, when Wagner determined definitively to separate from the burdensome Minna and enter into a relationship with the married Jessie Laussot (the couple planned to escape by ship to the Mideast), he sought to dispel her reservations about adultery by pointing out that on his side there was no question of a marriage in any case: the minister who had conducted it was, namely, a "Pietist," that is a sectarian, and thus had absolutely no jurisdiction in the matter.

Minna, who was promptly informed of this, swore (with heaven and hell her witnesses) to her marriage concluded before God and, deriving from it, to her legitimacy as Wagner's wife. For his part, he hastily explained it had all been a misunderstanding. Among other things, his back-pedaling led to the retreat of his presumptive future intended — heiress to millions and proto-type of his spouse-fleeing heroine Sieglinde — whereupon Wagner returned contritely to his wife in Zürich.

Scene 3

Between Peps and Papo

Wagner's Swiss exile, lasting nearly ten years, was marked by his conjugal life with an unloved wife, her

---

[148] Gregor-Dellin, p. 121.

The Laughing Wagner

equally unloved daughter Nathalie, nicknamed "Nette"—Minna gave out that she was her sister—and two warmly loved house pets, that were like his substitute children: the parrot Papo, and the lap dog Peps. From early on, Richard had evinced an affection for the animal world, above all for the barking, four-legged variety, whose familiar presence he would not forgo the rest of his life. He went so far as to design his Bayreuth gravesite such that he would lie beside his dogs.

During his time in Magdeburg, he kept a brown poodle who, as Glasenapp reports, numbered among his "truest, most blindly devoted friends."[149] The fact that the leading tenor at the City Theater was known by the nickname "Rüpel," and is addressed as "Dear Rüpel!"[150] in Wagner's letters did not keep the composer from dubbing his four-legged friend "Rüpel"[151] likewise, which led to odd confusions at rehearsal. After the barking poodle, "on account of some overly critical utterances" was banned from the orchestra pit, he used to wait every evening at the stage door for his master, the Music Director. "As if an emblem," it was reported, "the loyal Rüpel followed after him down every street and path as he went courting dressed in those days in a blue tail-coat and white vest."

The courtship in question, of course, was of Minna, with whose conduct the members of the theater company—unlike Wagner—were well acquainted. Not that they hesitated to enlighten him. When one of her colleagues, Madame Hacker, tried "to warn him away"

---

[149] Glasenapp, v. I, p. 234.
[150] *Ibid.*, v. I, p. 237.
[151] *Ibid.*, v. I, p. 234.

from his "Dulcinea," he cut her short with the light-hearted riposte: "Nothing means more to me than my poodle, my watch, and Minna Planer"[152]—in that order. The watch in question, he told Cosima years later, was a newly acquired silver one, and the matchless poodle, of course, the aforementioned Rüpel.

Unfortunately, the peculiarities of Minna's conduct apparently rubbed off on the dog. Once Wagner began avoiding his own living quarters on account of the almost daily court summonses from creditors nailed to his door, Rüpel, too, no longer saw himself bound to his unreliable master. One day, Wagner recounted, the poodle had "disappeared without a trace, which I saw as an evil omen of the total ruin of my situation."[153] After this melancholy experience, the abandoned dog owner purchased two black poodles, which out of spite he named "Dreck and Speck."[154]

The "total ruin of his situation" was still some way off: in the successive phases of his life, Wagner's financial descent evolved slowly at first, then with increasing velocity towards a crash, which Minna followed with growing panic. Their constant removal from place to place hinged directly on his creditors, whom he sought thus craftily to evade. From Magdeburg, they moved to distant Königsberg, where they were married, thence via detours (over which he read *Till Eulenspiegel*) to Riga, and from there, on an adventurous sea voyage that served him as inspiration for *The Flying Dutchman* to Paris, provisionally the nadir of his career. To be

---

[152] Cosima Wagner, *Diaries*, September 8, 1878.
[153] Wagner, *Mein Leben*, p. 129.
[154] Wagner, *Sämtliche Briefe*, v. I, p. 338. "*Dreck*"=dirt; "*Speck*"=bacon fat. The colloquialism means roughly "unwashed;" the words seem paired more for their rhyme than their sense.

sure, Wagner's creative successes, among them the operatic hit *Rienzi*, stood in welcome contrast to their material distress,.

Just when he could finally celebrate the triumph for which Minna had longed, thanks to this "grand opera" in Dresden, his accumulated debt paradoxically reached an absolute record high. Cynics insinuated it was also for this reason he so warmly embraced the insurrectionists around Mikhail Bakunin. In fact, at least for him, the failed revolution of 1849 brought about the desired result: leaving behind him debts amounting to 18,000 Thalers (for whose repayment, by his superior Lüttichau's delighted reckoning, he would have had to stay at his Dresden Kapellmeister's post for 32 years),[155] he departed for exile in Switzerland. No wonder he was in such a "pleasant" mood in Zürich, "like a dog who has escaped a whipping."[156]

Minna waited three months to see whether there might not be a chance after all for the wanted fugitive to return to his post and his pension rights. Then, heavy of heart, she resigned herself to following him. "Thus she announced to me," Wagner wrote later, "that she wished to arrive on a certain day in September of this year [1849] with the little dog Peps, the parrot Papo, and her sham 'sister' Nathalie at Rorschach on Swiss territory." Wagner, who went to meet them on foot, felt "actually quite moved when I saw the odd family, half of which consisted of house pets, land at the Rorschach harbor." His emotion was inspired less by wife and daughter than by the two other immigrants: "I have to

---

[155] Friederich Herzfeld, *Minna Planer und ihre Ehe mit Richard Wagner*, (Leipzig, 1938), p. 158.
[156] Herzfeld, p. 192.

concede candidly that the little dog and the bird had an especially favorable effect on me."[157]

"Little son Peps" with Little Wife. Minna Wagner with her husband's favorite dog during the Zürich exile, 1853, from a water-color by a female friend.

---

[157] Wagner, *Mein Leben*, p. 440.

This whimsical preference was not unfounded: the merry, if noisy little animal pair reminded him of the greatest success of his career so far. On that occasion even the critical Minna had been so enthused that on the night of the *Rienzi* premiere she had placed laurel leaves in her god-like spouse's bed so he might "rest on his laurels."[158] Witness to this scene of infrequent familial harmony had been a dog who since the first *Rienzi* rehearsal had displayed "passionate devotion" to the successful composer. In short, he gave the little animal the name "Peps," which pronounced with Saxon inflection sounded truly cozy.

Records are not in agreement about the dog's breed — whether it was a small spaniel or a Bolognese. Since a portrait of the animal on the lap of his mistress has fortunately survived,[159] both can probably be eliminated, while a glance at a catalogue of dog breeds would identify Peps as a member of the Papillon breed, descendant of the toy spaniel, in particular, the long-eared variety known as a Phalène. Prior to Wagner, Madame Pompadour and Marie Antoinette had both enjoyed this "nimble" as well as "self-possessed" animal.

If the little dog at his side thoroughly enjoyed the 1842 *Rienzi* triumph, a subsequent *Rienzi* fiasco was compensated for by another house pet. Thanks to the "most ludicrous, tawdry splendor" of the sets, the silly costumes, "borrowed from every conceivable fairy ballet in the wardrobe," and above all to the "aging, bloated, voiceless" leading man, the Hamburg premiere two years later resulted in a financial as well as an artistic disaster. The singer in the title role was "so

---
[158] Otto, p. 49
[159] Esther Drusche, *Richard Wagner*, (Leipzig, 1987), p. 88.

unbearable," Wagner recalled, "that I got the notion to have the Capitol collapse already in the second act, and bury him in its rubble."

Of course the Hamburg Theater Director registered the despondency of the composer, with whom he wished to remain on good terms. Wagner had mentioned to him how much his wife wanted a parrot, and "he knew how to arrange for a very engaging example of this avian species to come to me as a fringe benefit, as it were. I brought it with me in its narrow cage on the melancholy trip home, and was very moved when I saw that he returned my care for him with great and readily expressed attachment to me." Minna's reaction to the feathered gift proved enthusiastic. "So she received me with great joy," the husband reported, "for in this beautiful gray parrot it was palpable I was to make something of myself in the world."[160]

Wagner, Peps, and Papo became inseparable. The unreliable, though often trenchant Praeger reports even that Wagner could imitate Peps's bark and Papo's chattering perfectly,[161] so he could carry on an animated conversation with them. With their vociferous presence, two factions emerged in the Wagner household: one comprised the two ladies, who provided constant tension, the other, the two animals, who supplied a continuous din. It was this very counterpoint that rendered the nerve-wracking family life halfway bearable for the man of the house, since each source of turmoil was at the same time drowned out and to a certain extent neutralized by the other. In a facetious letter he wrote his Zürich friend from his travels, he confessed his longing for the animal

---

[160] Wagner, *Mein Leben*, p. 280.
[161] Praeger, p. 269.

contingent of the family, "whereby I do not deny that these children, granted me absent marital conception or birth through God's particular grace and mysterious providence, my little son Peps and my little daughter Papo, exercise a certain power of attraction over my inconstant nature."[162]

Though Peps was no talking dog, like E. T. A. Hoffmann's Berganza, Wagner had in its place Papo, a talking parrot, who could speak not only words but whole sentences flawlessly. Minna had taught him to say, "Richard Wagner, you are truly a great man!" a greeting surely not unwelcome to the recipient. But fearing this adulatory address might lead their guests to the wrong conclusion, Wagner modified the bird's praise self-ironically by producing his chatterbox for his guests and demanding "Why do you bark at the great Richard Wagner?"[163] Glasenapp, biographer under Cosima's supervision, hastened to assure his readers the Master had said this "with his inimitable irony." How ironic Wagner's observation may have been that "of all male creatures" Peps was "his best friend"[164] is, however, unrecorded.

On the other hand, that both animals prized physical proximity to the "great Richard Wagner" is amply documented. Especially the little dog, whose nervous sensibility had earned him the honorific "Peps the Agitated," because of his deep emotional dependency, never liked to leave his side. "There were times," Wagner wrote, "when one couldn't say a friendly word to him without triggering great howling and

---

[162] Wanger, *Sämtliche Briefe*, v. III, p. 234.
[163] Glasenapp, v. II, p. 180.
[164] *Bayreuther Festspielführer 1933*, p. 113.

sobbing,"[165] which might be faintly reminiscent of a certain "Bailiff Scrambled Egg."

In the Peps literature there is lack of unanimity as to which of the two, dog or master, valued the other's presence more highly during the process of composition. Wagner writes in his memoir that the dependency needs of the animal rose "often to the point of the burdensome," which manifested itself in its categorical imperative: "Peps was obliged always to lie behind me on the work-chair."[166] A contrasting narrative came from Marie, the daughter of Wagner's friend and set-designer Ferdinand Heine, who claimed that for this "white and brown spotted monster who tyrannized the household," Wagner had set up an "upholstered stool, on which Peps was obliged to lie, whenever the Master wished to compose. If the dog was not at hand, the entire household was mustered to search for him."[167]

Unlike Peps, Papo never went astray. If he was not to be seen, one could hear him. Incessantly chattering and singing, he gave evidence of his ever-presence, but never with the coarseness typical of his species. "He was so well-behaved," his master reported, not without pride, "that he never gave out an animalistic bird call, but only made himself heard speaking and singing."[168] Wagner, averse to all artificial restraint, had forgone caging the clever animal, and let him fly freely throughout the apartment, in which it "lived freely as

---

[165] Wagner, Mein Leben, p. 463.
[166] Ibid., p. 463.
[167] Richard Wagner, *Briefe. Die Sammlung Burrell*, (Frankfurt, 1953), p. 173.
[168] Wagner, *Mein Leben*, p. 463.

though in the trees."[169] If Papo had done something naughty, he would fly up high onto the curtain rods, and call to Wagner mockingly: "Come up, come up!"[170] Probably this tactic gave his master the idea for the speaking wood bird in *Siegfried*, who likewise instructs the hero to follow him.

Whenever Wagner entered the room—as Gustav Kietz recalled—he always went first "to the bird: he tipped his head, and the parrot stuck his head deep inside the wide collar between Wagner's shirt and neck and cuddled with his master."[171] If Wagner did not go up to the bird, the bird came to him: "If I stayed too long out of the living room, after repeated, vain calling of my name, 'Richard!' Papo usually fluttered to me in the study, where he positioned himself on the desk and often began busying himself excitedly with paper and pen."[172]

Wagner's Christian name was among Papo's first accomplishments; Minna employed him to call her husband to the table for meals. "When the soup was served, Minna instructed, 'Little Papo, call the master.'"[173] At the same time, the musically talented bird learned various melodies from *Rienzi*, Minna's favorite opera, from which he most often sang the uplifting "*Santo Spirito Cavaliere*," or the revolutionary "*Richard! Freiheit! Santo Spirito Cavaliere!*,"[174] which must have evoked the evanescence of fame and prosperity for the exiled artist.

---

[169] Otto, p. 60.
[170] Glasenapp, v. II, p. 547.
[171] *Ibid.*, v. II, p. 525.
[172] Wagner, *Mein Leben*, p. 463.
[173] Otto, p. 60.
[174] *Ibid.*, p. 60.

Over the long-term of his education, undertaken primarily by the lady of the house—which included the exclamation "The bad man, poor Minna!"[175]—his repertoire expanded to a breathtaking extent. Papo was like an autonomous music box giving forth favorite melodies. When Wagner returned home from rehearsal, the parrot met him most often with a snatch of Beethoven, "either with the great march theme from the last movement of the C minor Symphony, the opening measures of the Eighth Symphony in F major, or sometimes a festive theme from the *Rienzi* Overture."[176] Then he was permitted to stick his head into the shirt collar of his returning master.

When the parrot had finished entertaining his audience with classical tidbits, he switched over to all sorts of sound-mimicry that assumed the character of anticipatory echoes. "If he saw the people were about to clink their glasses, he imitated the sound of the glasses beforehand. If someone took out a handkerchief, he made the sound of blowing one's nose and clearing one's throat."[177] If the evening had advanced, Papo loved "to imitate the sound of a creaking door deceptively so that everyone instinctively turned to the look at the door,"[178] which may have been meant as a discreet hint from their host.

The sheer pleasure of making noise, though it might have annoyed humans in their vicinity, was common to all the Wagnerian parrots. Even in advanced age, Cosima had a grey parrot named Coco—also called Gockel—who could imitate a beer bottle's being

---

[175] *Ibid.*, p. 125.
[176] Wagner, *Mein Leben*, p. 463.
[177] Glasenapp, v. II, p. 547.
[178] Otto, p. 60.

opened, followed by the glug-glugging sound of its being drained, indeed as convincingly as the ensuing burp from the youngest Wagner daughter, Eva Chamberlain, to whom the mimicry emanating from the bird cage was more embarrassing than her chronic indisposition of involuntary burping itself.

The disturbing effect of his feathered housemates could prove a convenience to Wagner at times. If the presence of certain guests in the Wagner house was to be discouraged, Papo's successor, Jacquot (also called *Knackerchen*), would sing Leporello's "No rest, day or night,"[179] which could hardly be misconstrued. The Viennese music critic Eduard Hanslick, later Wagner's bitterest enemy, wrote of a visit during the Dresden years during which "Wagner's conversation, which I would gladly have heard undisturbed, was constantly accompanied and drowned out by the awful squawking of a parrot. 'How can you stand this racket,' I asked. 'Oh, I am quite used to it,' Wagner shouted, laughing. 'He is a good little creature whom I take with me everywhere. It's true he's often noisy.'" Whereupon followed the pointed witticism: "On the other hand, I'm blessed to have a wife who doesn't play the piano."[180]

At about the same time, in 1845, another music critic, Karl Gaillard, found his pleasure at Wagner piano pieces spoiled by the joint cacophony of Papo and Peps. He complained especially about "the rending of the most effective moments in these [pieces] by the yapping of his small, unbelievably spoiled canine favorite, or the absurd notes of his parrot calling out in the middle of an inspired performance of the *Pilgrim's Chorus* or

---

[179] Weißheimer, p. 28.
[180] Otto, p. 74.

Elsa's declaration of love, 'Richard, come up here!', or remarkably imitating the shrill sound of clinking glasses."[181] It may well have been that Papo with his "absurd notes" was simply expressing what his master was just then thinking.

Though Minna was their primary teacher, Wagner also made important contributions to the growth of the parrot's repertoire. Thus, when he was staying with the Zwickauer family he reported to her concerning the "progress" in Jacquot's training in enunciation that he was not shy about colloquialisms: "He's mastered 'thunderation!' now."[182] The following year on June 11, 1855 while the composer was concertizing in London—notwithstanding a Royal Saxon warrant out for his arrest—he was granted the honor of a gracious reception by Queen Victoria, who bestowed a royal commendation. He hastened to inform Minna in a letter of the interesting details of their conversation.

"Oh God, Dear Mienel," he wrote her, "I am quite hoarse from much talking-with-the-Queen! First she asked me how Peps was doing, then, whether Knackerchen was well-behaved." Since they were already on nearly familiar terms, the Queen—"she is *not* fat, but very short and not pretty at all, with an unfortunately somewhat red nose"—had made a modest request: "The Queen had heard of my beautiful satin trousers—might I send them to her at the palace so the Prince Consort Albert could have a similar pair made from their pattern?"[183]

---

[181] *Ibid.*, p. 67.
[182] Wagmer. *Sämtliche Briefe*, v. VI, p. 211. The epithet was the German commonplace *"Donnerwetter!"*
[183] *Ibid.*, v. VII, p. 216.

Three days later, Wagner went a step further, though it remains unclear whether the conventional Minna might not have taken his little joke seriously. "Opinions still differ," he reported to her, "over how I might have made such an advantageous impression on the Queen. Praeger maintains I looked so splendid wearing his white cravat that she was smitten with me; others claim it was the beautiful Zürich tailcoat. For my part, I reproach myself for having betrayed her throughout the entire concert. She was supposedly under the stubborn illusion that I had new gloves on, whereas they were only freshly washed. You will recognize my thrift here, but unfortunately also a want of forthrightness. By the way, I am hoping to get my satin trousers back from the palace soon; hopefully the Prince won't have tried them on, the thought of which makes me squeamish."[184]

It would be a fundamental mistake to imagine the little man surrounded himself only with correspondingly little dogs—aside from Dreck and Speck, Peps and Fips, as Peps's successors were named, there were also Koss, Schnauz, and Putz. Most were large, some huge. While still in Riga, Wagner had wanted to keep a wolf, which would have threatened domestic peace; instead, he acquired a coal-black Newfoundland by the name of Robber, an intimidatingly gigantic breed, to which in the persons of his later companions, Russ, Marke, and Brange he remained true. Nor was his devoted hunting dog Pohl exactly small, named after his most devoted admirer, Richard Pohl, from Baden-Baden, who styled himself "the earliest Wagnerian." The composer was so devoted to his Pohl—the dog, not the Wagnerian—that his assistant Hans von Bülow remarked facetiously in

---

[184] *Ibid.*, v. VII, p. 225.

1866, "Wagner's wife is dead, and his dog Pohl likewise."[185]

Occasionally also smaller dogs were advantageous who did not, like Wagner's black-coated and powerfully voiced monster, attract general attention. For instance, Wagner found his little Fips, whom his Zürich inamorata Mathilde Wesendonck had given him, quite practical. The little Bolognese proved himself to be quick to learn, and uninhibited. "When I stood up from a meal," Wagner reported to his wife, "he jumped immediately onto my chair to lick the plate."[186] But he had other talents as well. If on their usual morning stroll his master had a sudden call of nature with which he had "to deal" behind a tree, Fips would stand guard. "As soon as he heard someone coming from afar, he would bark, giving me time to clear out."[187]

For the sake of completeness, the poodle Putz must also be mentioned, who enhanced Wagner's Bayreuth Newfoundland economy with his "Putzness."[188] Belonging to the noble breed of the "Scottish Silk Poodle," he was dubbed admiringly the "dog from the land of the fairies"[189] by Wagner. But this dog emanated not from Hoffmann's fantasies, but as a gift from the Wagnerite Count Krockow. In a poem of thanks, his idol put in the aristocrat's mouth the rhyme: "From Scotland, here comes a poodle – 'a gift in return for your noodling.'"[190]

---

[185] Glasenapp, v. IV, p. 160.
[186] Wagner, *Sämtliche Briefe*, v. IX, p. 238.
[187] *Ibid.*, v. VIII, p. 71.
[188] An untranslatable pun. "*Putzigkeit*": the quality of being cute and amusing.
[189] Cosima Wagner, *Diaries*, July 20, 1873.
[190] Wagner, *Sämtliche Schriften und Dichtungen*, v. XVI, p. 227. "*Von*

By "noodling," he must have meant *The Ring of the Nibelung*.

Scene 4

Fantasy Pieces in Callot's Manner

The question presents itself whether Wagner communicated his passion for acrobatics to his clever little dogs. In other words, could Dreck, Speck, Peps, Fips, and the gang stand on their hind legs like little men, do summersaults, or jump through hoops? Nothing like that is known. Wagner did not believe in training. His pinschers, poodles, and giant dogs were brought up in an anti-authoritarian manner. In his own words: "When I whistle to the dogs, they whistle back."[191]

The extraordinary affection of his four-legged friends for him surely derived from the fact that he let every dog be its own master. When a visitor to Wahnfried spoke of the remarkable empathy of the dogs, who seemed to read his own mood at any moment from their master's bearing, Wagner's response was that "Brange and Marke should immediately be let in, so they could make the experiment."[192]

Only Robber, the giant dog from Riga, is known to have mastered something useful: he loved diving for things. After accompanying the Wagners by ship and post coach through half of Central Europe, he found his way around the huge city of Paris more quickly than his

---

Schottland kommt ein Pudel: 'Der sei für dein Gedudel!'"
[191] Cosima Wagner, *Diaries*, December 10, 1878.
[192] *Ibid.*,

master. He chose a pool in the gardens of the Palais-Royal as his favorite spot, among other things because there he "could enjoy the company of many other dogs."

But Robber's real hobby consisted in entertaining the assembled idlers "by his fetching from the pool pond there." On promenades, "he usually begged us for permission to go swimming," his master wrote, "and soon drew a so rapidly growing crowd of spectators, which, with boisterous shouts of delight, relished his diving and bringing up all sorts of sunken articles of clothing and implements."[193] Until the police put an abrupt end to his performances.

Just as abruptly, the love between Robber and the composer came to an end. Following one of his solitary excursions, Wagner reported, "he failed to return home." As in the case of Rüpel's abandonment, his master's increasingly inauspicious finances seem to have caused the Newfoundland to cast about for a solider situation. For Wagner's flight from his old creditors had only led him circumstantially into the hands of new ones, since the expected miracle of ascending directly from the threat of an Estonian debtors' prison into the Parisian operatic empyrean had evaporated.

On the one hand, the composer himself viewed his two and a half year rejection by the city as an existential catastrophe, in which the perennially complaining Minna could only reinforce him. On the other, he took solace in his conviction that he was an unrecognized genius, whose greatest hardships must be behind him. One thing he knew for sure: his suffering stemmed

---

[193] Wagner, *Mein Leben*, p. 188.

only from Paris's failure to realize with whom it was dealing. Not his own inadequacy was to blame for the string of humiliations and setbacks, but rather the inability of this infinitely vain, narcissistic city to recognize his genius.

Then the miracle he no longer thought possible occurred. On his daily round of solicitation through the streets of the metropolis[194] he was recognized after all: suddenly "someone greeted him, and he was so happy to have been known and greeted by any soul there that he returned the greeting with excessive courtesy, but then racked his brains over who it might have been, and after much effort finally recalled the servant of Mme. Viardot, which 'terribly annoyed' him."[195] "Annoyed" because the renowned singer Pauline Viardot-Garcia, from whom he had hoped to acquire support, had just returned his French songs to him; "terribly" because he had mistaken a servant's livery for the uniform of a general.

Fortunately, even in Paris life was not wholly without its humorous side. As recorded in *Mein Leben*, to save on heating costs the Wagners had set up a one-room household: the bedroom converted to a "living-room, dining-room, and study," with the advantage that "with two steps from the bed," the study desk could be reached, "from which I then turned the chair around to the dining table, and stood up from it fully only to go back to bed late in the evening."[196] The shoemaker's fees, too, were spared: "Around this time I often and with cheerful pride showed off my boots, which at last still gave literally just the illusion of dressing for my

---

[194] Wagner, *Sämtliche Schriften und Dichtungen*, v. XVI, p. 185.
[195] Cosima Wagner, *Diaries*, February 24, 1871.
[196] Wagner, *Mein Leben*, p. 201.

feet, because finally the soles had completely disappeared."[197]

In the innumerable letters he sent home begging for money and favors, Wagner pulled out all the stops of gallows humor, as for example when he wrote to Robert Schumann, "I'm doing marvelously, considering I've not yet starved to death,"[198] or to Giacomo Meyerbeer concerning the "threnody" of his life "that one day—I have not the slightest doubt—when I will have become amazingly famous, I am sure to be celebrated and lamented by some great poet in 24 to 48 songs."[199]

He hoped for true miracles from his much envied model Giacomo Meyerbeer, who, if one is to believe Heinrich Heine, achieved his sensational Paris success by skillfully spreading money around. For the satirist wrote that the composer of *Les Huguenots* would "be immortal as long as he lived. And even a bit longer, because he has paid in advance."[200] Wagner would also gladly have paid something in advance if he had only had the means. To acquire both money and fame with Meyerbeer's help, he presented a sample of his compositional art to his countryman who had achieved success abroad.

After thoughtful study, Meyerbeer began lauding his young colleague extravagantly, though not, to be sure, as Wagner had hoped. Instead of the score's musical quality, the successful composer of grand opera singled out Wagner's penmanship in his fair copy for praise.

---

[197] *Ibid.*, p. 215.
[198] Wagner, *Sämtliche Briefe*, v. I, p. 428.
[199] *Ibid.*, v. I, p. 378.
[200] Glasenapp, v. II, p. 87.

Later, the reluctant copyist complained, only half in jest, "This act of admiration has become a curse— for the rest of my earthly life, I will have to produce perfect copies of my scores!"[201]

As pretty much everything else Wagner undertook to further his career went off the rails, his *Columbus Overture*, too, suffered shipwreck in the reception of its Paris audience—which ought not to have surprised him since six years earlier in Magdeburg the piece had "filled all its hearers with terror." This time, too, the problem lay with the massive forces of trumpets to whom the composer had entrusted the depiction of "the promised land for which the hero's searching eye was scanning."[202] Unfortunately, this theme, speaking from the heart of the artist, could not convincingly be communicated to the Parisians, in consequence of which, scarcely a hand stirred in applause when Columbus happily had discovered the New World.

Afterwards (Wagner wrote with self-conscious pomposity), those in the know assured him "that my Overture, though it might bore the whole world, would nonetheless surely have been applauded, had not the unfortunate trumpet players' regularly missing the notes in the bravura passages incited the audience to just barely suppressed disapprobation; because Parisians, for the most part, listen attentively only for the virtuosic parts of a performance, like, for instance, the successful production of certain notoriously treacherous notes."[203] Wagner's indignation over the rudeness of the audience was so great that for the rest

---

[201] Wagner, *Sämtliche Briefe*, v. VI, p. 151
[202] Wagner, *Mein Leben*, p. 105.
[203] *Ibid.*, p. 203.

of his life he was annoyed by the mocking of botched trumpet notes, so-called "squeaks."[204]

For the sake of the daily baguette, the immigrant was compelled to set aside his own creations, for which there was no demand, and instead dream up carnival melodies for the dance cabarets, here called "vaudeville," or arrange popular opera melodies in the manner of his Dresden mentor, Flachs, for the use of amateurs, or even doll up for use elsewhere his sketch for *The Flying Dutchman*, on whose composition he was already at work. In any case, he weathered this uninterrupted string of humiliations brilliantly, thanks to his reliable sense of humor, and also to the satisfaction of his customers.

There were exceptions. Toward the end of his time in Paris he met an old acquaintance, the "by no means witless Jewish musician and composer" Josef Dessauer, who planned just the sort of striking breakthrough at the Grand Opera that Wagner had himself vainly dreamed of. Since this "hypochondriacal odd bird"[205] had come into money, he commissioned his hardship-tested friend, against payment of a considerable sum, to write an appropriate libretto for him, preferably in the style of *The Flying Dutchman*.

"This time," Wagner recalled, "I rifled my memories of Hoffmann, and easily hit on the treatment of *The Mines of Falun*. Truly, I was successful in working up this wonderful material exactly as I had imagined, and

---

[204] "*Gickser*," in the current parlance of Anglophone brass players, "clams." See also "Epilogue," and n. 551, p. 251.
[205] Wagner, *Sämtliche Schriften und Dichtungen*, v. XVI, p. 60.

Dessauer, too, was convinced this subject was worth his trouble of setting it to music."[206]

Unfortunately, both were mistaken. They had overlooked the Paris convention that the ballet intermezzi were at least as important as the opera itself, due mostly to the custom among male opera-goers of taking as mistresses precocious members of the *corps de ballet*, so-called "rats," whom they wished to see onstage as often and as scantily clad as possible. The Theater Director's importunities notwithstanding, Wagner was not prepared to make a danceable adaptation of the subterranean "Mines." It speaks well for his intransigence in this instance that even 20 years later, when he mounted his *Tannhäuser* in Paris in 1860, he still disdained the viewing prejudices of the male cohort of his audience, for which he suffered the consequent debacle.

In another point, too, the stubbornness with which Wagner pursued his ideas—often over the course of decades—revealed itself. A highlight of E. T. A. Hoffmann's narrative material, the seductive mountain queen in the crystal palace, was to reappear in *Tannhäuser* as the seductress Venus in the grotto of love, where, addressed by her lover as "queen," she is surrounded by dancers in an erotic ballet. Another musically charming *pièce de resistance* of the Dessauer assignment reappears in *The Ring*, where the hammer-blows of the approaching Hoffmannesque mountain spirits, sounding from afar to great effect, are echoed in the rhythmic rising and falling din of Nibelung hammers.

---

[206] Wagner, *Mein Leben*, p. 224.

Despite the disaster of his opera project, Josef Dessauer did not give up. Having already paid Wagner, he had the idea of asking him to write the text to an oratorio about the great sinner Mary Magdalene. This, too, was destined never to come to fruition. "Since on the very day he made me this request," Wagner wrote, "he was struck with an especially debilitating attack of hypochondria (he claimed he had seen his own head lying in front of his bed that morning), I didn't turn his request down, but asked for more time, which I regret to say I have remained determined to take even to this present day."[207]

Wagner scholarship has long debated how seriously we are to take the composer's in part comically lachrymose, in part tragically despairing complaints voiced against prospective benefactors. There has also been much speculation over whether the composer actually spent several days in the Paris debtors' prison, as his wife broadcast in letters to underscore her appeals for credit. Scholarship generally thinks not. Perhaps Wagner's Paris Calvary even in other respects was not quite so grim as it appears in his Jeremiads. Noteworthy, at all events, is that already soon after their return home, Minna felt great longing for Paris. And accounts from the circle of their bohemian friends there, whose undisputed focal point the master raconteur, musician, and wit Wagner had been, offer a not so devastating picture of the "years of misery and hunger." One struggled, yes, but had fun in the process.

At any rate, the young composer was privileged to be accepted into the illustrious Paris circle around Heinrich Heine, although the great satirist, in response

---

[207] *Ibid.*, p. 225.

to the illusions of the younger man, had "piously folded his hands."[208] Meyerbeer's patronage of Wagner seemed "suspicious" to Heine because it seemed already to prove "that he had no talent."[209] When Wagner approached this countryman, too, for money, the poet proved generous, offering help in the form of both cash and credit. All in all, the "credit genius," as Thomas Mann dubbed him, seems even in Paris never to have been so wretched that he abandoned his sense of humor, not to mention his sense of mission.

The best summation of the Paris intermezzo is a caricature by his friend Ernst Benedikt Kietz. It is no coincidence that its grotesque tableau of figures is reminiscent of the French illustrator Jacques Callot, to whom E. T. A. Hoffmann had dedicated his famous *Fantasy Pieces in Callot's Manner* — among them, *The Golden Pot*. No coincidence either that while Kietz worked on his "Great Caricature of Paris Suffering," providing "several bottles of rum" as a substitute for firewood, Wagner read *Tales of Hoffmann* aloud for the artist and Minna.[210]

In the middle of the drawing, created "to our delight," we see the Master as musical jack-of-all-trades: with one hand he plays the piano, which carries the inscription "infernal machine," while the other energetically beats the tympani. The feet too are subject to division of labor: the left foot operates a cymbal and the right a piano pedal. In order to coax mice and rats as well as notes from a church organ, Wagner is riding on a bellows, and on close inspection, one discovers

---

[208] Joachim Köhler, *Der Letzte der Titanen*, (Munich, 2001), p. 182.
[209] *Ibid.*, p. 184.
[210] Wagner, *Mein Leben*, p. 214.

two trumpets apparently being sounded by means of his own corporal wind.

"Paris Illusions." In Ernst Benedikt Kietz's grotesque 1840/41 drawing, Wagner, musical Jack-of-all-trades, with tears of emotion streaming from his eyes, accompanies the singing duo of wife Minna and dog Robber, on tympani, piano, trumpets, and organ.

Minna, singing in her nightgown, as *mater dolorosa*, wears a crown of thorns atop her nightcap, and holds the sheet-music from which the virtuoso is playing the dreadful piece so earnestly. In the foreground are sacks of gold with the inscription "negative wealth" printed with multiple zeros, and Brueghelesque toads, snakes, and a monstrous cockroach in Wagner's jacket pocket. Visible too is an enema bag, and the sole of his right boot full of holes. As if by way of consolation, an imaginary audience cheers for *Rienzi*. Appropriate musical accompaniment is being played in heaven above them by a Hoffmannesque ghost orchestra, ringing out its caterwaul with a bass viol bowed with a saw, a trumpet-playing devil, and a violin-playing Death. A small inscription epitomizes the message of the grotesque: "Paris Illusions."

Two Wagnerian canines are also immortalized in the picture. Above, in heaven, a music-making little dog is making proper noise with cymbals and resembles Peps, although he was born only after Wagner's return to Dresden. Unmistakably recognizable, though, is Robber, for he carries his name on his broad breast. The black-pelted Newfoundland sits beside Wagner's piano and howls, as though already determined, as biographer Gregor-Dellin wrote, "to look around for something better"[211] or, as his master claimed, to be abducted by sinister forces.

Novelistically, Wagner described his surprising reunion with his dog, which in retrospect seemed to him a terrible omen. The musician was again out on his rounds seeking funds, or, as he called it, going "begging." "The streets were blanketed by a thick fog, and as I stepped out of the house, the first thing I recognized was my dog Robber, abducted from me a year before. I thought at first I was seeing a ghost, but called to him quickly in a shrill voice; the animal knew

---

[211] Gregor-Dellin, p. 144.

me instantly and approached quite near. But when I stepped toward him rapidly with outstretched arm, it was as though all other memory was overwhelmed in the equally surprised animal by the fear of punishment such as I had foolishly administered to him several times during the last period of our life together. He backed away from me fearfully, and when I ran after him quickly, he ran ever faster away from me." Wagner pursued him "like a madman," through a maze of streets hardly negotiable in the fog, until, "dripping with sweat and breathless [I] lost sight [of him] forever." For a time, he stood as though transfixed, staring into the fog. "Deeply shaken, knees trembling, I took up once more my sorry business."[212]

Surprisingly, Wagner's career got going after all, though not in the opera Mecca of Paris, but rather in his hometown, whose court theater offered him a position. "Comprehending the language of reason and of the stomach," Heinrich Heine wrote mockingly, Wagner "wisely gave up the treacherous project of establishing himself on the French stage," whereupon he "flapped back to the German potato land."[213] Whether the poet chose this unusual conceit because he viewed Wagner as flighty, or because he knew Wagner had once been known as Geyer[214] can no longer be determined.

In October, 1842, a half year after Wagner's return to the "potato land," the opera performance dreamed up in Kietz's caricature became a reality, and to top it off, *Rienzi* made its composer famous overnight. To be sure, it did not make him rich. The composer received 300 Thaler, which registered beside the silver armor of

---

[212] Wagner, *Mein Leben*, p. 199.
[213] Otto, p. 46.
[214] i.e., "vulture."

his titular hero that had cost 400 Thaler, amounted more nearly to an expense reimbursement. Nevertheless, in the years following, Wagner's career enjoyed a terrific upswing, whose high points were the premieres of *The Flying Dutchman* and *Tannhäuser*, until finally, eight years after his return from Paris, the meteoric rise ended in revolution and a wanted poster.

Somehow Wagner had sensed from the outset that the position of Court Kapellmeister with its aristocratic livery and its protocol of hierarchy was not his dish of tea. To Minna's great satisfaction, the position yielded sufficient income. But to debts newly accumulated were immediately added old ones Wagner thought he had escaped with his flight from Riga. So demands for payment arrived from every stage of the course of his life, "even from my student, my high-school days, so that occasionally I cried out in bewilderment, I suppose I will now also get a bill from my wet-nurse for suckling."[215]

Just a few weeks after arrival in Dresden, he felt, like Minna, a quiet homesickness for the Seine. The passionate outdoorsman and acrobat who, like his hero Siegfried, preferred being alone in nature with a couple of nice animals, wrote to Samuel Lehrs, his fellow in suffering left behind in Paris, that he had already had enough of this all too "pleasant" life among his countrymen — "a damned lot, these Saxons." "How I shudder to think," he wrote of his melancholy prospects, "that once a banal, boring, 'good fortune' fell to my lot, in which, instead of chickens and goats, I should have to find pleasure in privy councilors and asses!" Clearly his move had not brought him what he

---

[215] Wagner, *Mein Leben*, p. 261.

had hoped for after all. "Paris, Dresden, or Schilda — it's a matter of indifference to me forever . . . there are whole days on which I don't give a damn about my operas."[216]

As became evident, he soon had enough of his next way-station, too. In Zürich, not just Minna and Nette, but also the comfortable provincial bourgeoisie got on his nerves. From time to time, he sought rest and recuperation in France, and found them in a small town outside the metropolis, where the "chickens" that were essential to his happiness were no mere figure of speech. Wagner truly had a weakness for this feathered creature, which, as he once joked cornily, always made for a good "pick-nick," because while it pecked, it also nodded.[217]

In a country inn where he sought "in bread, cheese, and a bottle of wine to refresh" himself, something surprising happened. "A flock of hens gathered around me, to whom I diligently threw pieces of my bread. I was touched to see the selfless restraint with which the rooster yielded up all the food to his little wives, despite my throwing pieces expressly to him. The hens growing ever bolder, however, flew onto my table, and laid fearlessly into my food. The rooster, now, flew after them and when he saw that everything was in a confused mess, he threw himself with pent-up appetite onto the cheese. When I saw myself finally driven completely away from the table by this flapping confusion, a great merriment came over me for the first time in a long while. I had to laugh out-loud and looked

---

[216] Wagner, *Sämtliche Briefe*, v. II, p. 101.
[217] Cosima Wagner, *Diaries*, November 15, 1878. An untranslatable pun he set his children as a riddle: *"Welche sind die Tiere, die immer Picknick machen? Die Hühner, sie picken und nicken dazu!"*

The Laughing Wagner

around for the sign of the inn."[218] This in turn gave birth to even greater hilarity, for the owner's name was "Homo," human in German. Wagner took this and the comical poultry as a "sign from fate: at all costs I must seek my lodging here."

Wagner, who had to have whatever struck his fancy, was so impressed that from that moment on a flock of hens constituted an element of his ideal lifestyle, and not just on account of the eggs. When he returned to Paris in 1860, he visited an animal exposition where he found a fine specimen of a rooster. Although "without a penny" in his pocket, he was determined to purchase this rooster "at a cost of 800 Francs . . . If I owned him, I thought, I would seem like really something to myself."[219] An unconscious motive may have played a role in his curious wish: an expression he often used to express comically his notorious lack of success was, "No rooster crows for me." If he could call it his own, at least this misfortune would be rectified.

With success came the rooster. Behind the Tribschen estate near Lucerne, which Ludwig II provided for Wagner, there lived a colorful menagerie with turkey cock ("surely the prototype of the sailing ships"[220]), pigeons, and a pair of golden pheasants given him by the King, named Wotan and Fricka after the married couple of *The Ring*. The numerous flock of hens was ruled over by a "splendid Calcutta rooster,"[221] who, as Cosima noted, performed his morning wake-up duties "most valiantly," and conveyed to Wagner regularly the sense of finally being "something."

---

[218] Wagner, *Mein Leben*, p. 453.
[219] Cosima Wagner, *Diaries*, June 1, 1878.
[220] *Ibid.*, May 1, 1872.
[221] Glasenapp, v. IV, p. 238.

Homage of the Animal Kingdom. In 1879, after Wagner had published a passionate appeal against animal experimentation, the cartoonist of *Der Schalk* satirized him by showing Lohengrin's swan and the dragon Fafner, among others, paying him homage.

There is more: he and his family were always seeking to recognize new quotations from his works in the warbled notes of the hens. In Tribschen, it was the morning crowing of a dwarf rooster named Giölnir — translated, "all-crushing" — in which Wagner, still dreaming, thought he heard "the Siegfried motif, slightly modified, on a toy trumpet."[222] Hearing the crowing of a Bayreuth rooster, Cosima remarked "that

---

[222] Cosima Wagner, *Diaries*, September 20, 1869.

The Laughing Wagner

he [was sounding] the call of the trombones from the second act of *Lohengrin*."[223] And the following day, the children, who joined in the amusing game of guessing the melodies, claimed that "one of the roosters had sung from the 'Siegfried Idyll!'"[224]

Having fulfilled his dream of a personal festival theater and a private villa in Bayreuth, one last heart's desire remained still to be realized. In 1878, while working on *Parsifal*, Wagner took his family purposefully to visit an agricultural exhibition. "The roosters in particular," Cosima noted, "give Richard much pleasure. A rooster with a splendid comb reminds him, by his emphatically nervous movements, of Berlioz; another's tangled comb calls to mind Beethoven's unruly hair. All this multi-colored crowing amuses him greatly. He wants a flock like that."[225]

Wagner was so enthusiastic over the fulfillment of his dream that he invited several friends to the dedication of his chicken coop, and "decreed" that breakfast was to be served in front of the new shed. On this festive occasion, according to Cosima, "the birds [were] enthroned"[226] (whatever we are to take that to mean). "But we laughed ourselves silly over Wagner's effervescence and jokes," his old friend Malwida von Meysenbug recalled. "His high spirits welled from every pore . . . This morning there was a party in the garden, the new chicken coop was finished, and Wagner brought out a bunch of his rare hens who were

---

[223] *Ibid.*, August 28, 1878.
[224] *Ibid.*, August 29, 1878.
[225] *Ibid.*, June 1, 1878.
[226] *Ibid.*, August 30, 1878.

now turned out freely for the first time." In short: "Wagner was quite content with his hens."[227]

With a particular rooster, too, it seems. If Cosima had heard correctly, "so melancholy a cry" rang out in the morning from one of the roosters, "that it reminded me of the opening of the prelude" to *Parsifal*. Wagner, reminded perhaps of Papo's mimicry, seemed not in the slightest surprised. "Richard says "he knows what I mean," Cosima continues; "it is true; it is that diminished fifth that sounds so distinctive, he will call it the rooster motif."[228]

From her final diary entry on the subject of chickens, a scant half year before Wagner's death, we can infer that her husband knew first and foremost how to see the amusing aspects of these feathered creatures. "Around noontime I hear him in the garden laughing loudly," she writes on September 6, 1882. "It was over the noise the hens were making laying their eggs."

Yet one more feathered favorite must be recalled: the Sicilian owl, who during Wagner's last vacation in Palermo just a year before his death, had his family on tenterhooks for weeks. Wagner had discovered him in the garden of a certain family Florio, where in an aviary the "captive show-owl," according to Cosima, "aroused his profound admiration." "There we have nature!" Wagner cried confronting the mute raptor perched there, "without pretense, tooth and claw, but true." As a likeness, oddly, only the king of beasts occurred to him. "Like a lion," he cried, yes "this fellow is more beautiful than a lion!" He remained long sunk in contemplation of the owl, and after viewing the rest of

---

[227] Otto., p. 568.
[228] Cosima Wagner, *Diaries*, November 1, 1878.

the garden, "he returned to him. He laughed over the clarity of its call," which seemed to remind him of his parrots. "It's as though he is learning to talk."

From then on, Cosima reports, he made his way on walks to the show-owl, and there developed—as was usual in Wagner's relations to animals—" between him and the bird a kind of friendship that strengthened and grew in attachment with each reunion."[229]

How great the grief when, on a solitary walk, Cosima found the aviary empty, "and learned the beautiful bird was dead." Wagner was inconsolable. "'He was pining for us,' was Wagner's initial outcry when he learned of it; then we consoled ourselves with the thought of how miserable a life this beautiful creature must have led imprisoned in his cage."

After a few days of silent grief Cosima had the idea of "having the noble animal, whose sight had given the Master such pleasure, stuffed as a lasting memorial to take back with him to Bayreuth." Wagner's factotum, the barber Schnappauf, was sent to collect the corpse.

Things played out otherwise, though. When the Bayreuth eccentric inquired discreetly of the Florio family with respect to the deceased, "whether his remains [were] still well [enough] preserved" for him to be stuffed, the servant replied he was very sorry ("*mi dispiace molto*"). It was not the owl who had died, but Signior Florio's mother-in-law."[230]

---

[229] Glasenapp, v. VI, p. 545.
[230] Cosima Wagner, *Diaries*, February 13. 1882.

Act III

The "Seven Wonders of the World"

*"Children, don't hold it against me! True,
I wrote it that way; it sounds awful all the same!"*[231]

Scene 1

The Sorrows of the "Young Tin-pot Potentate"

The notion that the jocular Wagner was the "true" Wagner seems enormously attractive, especially in contrast to his works, which hardly seem light-hearted. It is, however, no more tenable than the view that he was entirely a gilt-edged classic, on the one hand, or simply, in Thomas Mann's choice formulation, a "shabby character" on the other. This latter version of the "true" Wagner also proves fruitful, since nothing is easier to describe than another person's faults. Make no mistake: anyone examining Wagner's rap-sheet will certainly turn up plenty, and the more closely he trains his microscope, the more sins will be revealed to his searching eye.

Atop the list is the way he vented his aversion to others. Wagner was prone to exacting revenge, be it against individuals who had incurred his displeasure, or with ethnic groups like the Jews, whom he held accountable for his failures. But he often carried this out — surprising as it may seem — as "the Laughing Wagner,"

---

[231] Philippi, p. 122.

not with irony, to be sure, but with sarcasm, malicious and gloating. At such times, the genuinely liberating laughter he usually provoked in those around him, turned to the oppressive laughter of mockery, such as he wrote unmistakably into the roles of his arch-villain Alberich and his cynical chief of the gods, Wotan.

The conundrum how the creator of those "Seven Wonders of the World" could have lowered himself to a level that at times stigmatizes him as a moral borderline case cannot be explained by psychological, sociological, or even specifically national peculiarities. Paradoxically, it is tied up with his creative gift and its astonishing "wonder works," which — precisely — evoked but a small measure of astonishment and admiration. Instead of bringing him the well-deserved rewards of fame and fortune the ambitious artist had expected, they offered a growing number of observers occasions for sarcasm, scorn, and gloating, which rendered their victim not famous, but infamous, and left in their wake a serious ebb in his finances. In other words, try as he might, he was mocked, while his financial troubles mounted as though of their own accord.

It would be hard to find an example in cultural history in which as highly gifted an artist was the target of such entrenched persecution. Since the obloquy most often wore the guise of the humorous, it escaped the moral censure that it sought to destroy a person. One wished "merely" to deliver him (whose outward appearance even provoked mirth) up to well-deserved ridicule. This came easily insofar as by his physiognomy, dress, and eccentric behavior he himself left openings for satirical treatment. And still more by his art that took the "liberty" of simply jettisoning tried and true rules, and putting its own in their place, which with a provocative air he had the added arrogance to raise to the status of universal standard.

The art establishment and the critical class, who were not prepared to be lectured to by an anarchistic "musician of the future," were indeed provoked. In his *Meistersinger*, Wagner had this depressing scenario play out with the triumph of his avant-garde Walther von Stolzing. In his own life there could be no talk of triumph. The perennial laughter of scorn soured his every success.

Not just the critics made fun of him. A patronizing condescension, even a smugly dismissive posture had set in among the prominent cultural leaders of his day too, which in the truest sense made a mockery of Wagner's abilities. "Since my return from exile, I have encountered in Germany on all sides the sole concern," thus his sarcastic balance sheet, "of keeping away from me."[232] There were to be sure some, like the Swiss writer Gottfried Keller, who conceded he was "a very talented person," but added that there was "a bit of the Figaro and charlatan,"[233] about him — which for sheer bourgeois venom could hardly be topped. The popular novelist Karl Gutzkow characterized the composer as virtually the "Cagliostro of the day's music,"[234] in saying which he joined together two deprecatory slurs of currency, namely first that Wagner was a devious confidence man, and second that he cared only for quick success. Future Nobel Prize winning author Paul Heyse assured his readers that Wagner's dubious arts

---

[232] Glasenapp, *Wagner-Ezyklopädie*, v. I, p. 224.
[233] Gregor-Dellin, p. 405.
[234] Wilhelm Tappert, *Wörterbuch der Unhöflichkeit*, (Munich, 1967), p 28.

were accepted only because he "led the poor dim souls around by the nose."[235]

"Musical Worthlessness." In London Wagner was regularly torn apart by segments of the press, both as conductor and composer — here, a caricature from *Vanity Fair*, 1877.

His musical colleagues, who knew perfectly well how to assess this supposed adventurer, did their best to belittle him. Robert Schumann carped that he was not a

---

[235] *Ibid.*, p. 28.

good musician, that he lacked a sense of form and euphony.[236] Hector Berlioz declared him "obviously mad."[237] Even Tchaikovsky couldn't suppress the exclamation "What a Don Quixote this Wagner is!"[238] satirizing Wagner's tragicomic penchant for solitary combat. Heinrich Dorn, who had once conducted Wagner's "Tympani Stroke Symphony" into the ground, affirmed that the composer had the ego of a "Dalai Lama."[239] And Moritz Hauptmann, respected Kantor of St. Thomas Church, Leipzig, delivered the fateful verdict following a performance of the *Tannhäuser* overture that it was "quite horrible, incomprehensibly clumsy, long and boring."[240] These, and other such flashes of genius, a list which could be extended indefinitely, Wagner had to register and process, which—since he was also intellectually an acrobatic roly poly—he was surprisingly successful in doing.

It was only his deep-seated aversion to the two celebrity composers of his time— though cloaked at times in a show of friendship—that he never overcame. Giacomo Meyerbeer, whose powerful success with audiences despite his modest gifts he envied, and Felix Mendelssohn Bartholdy, whose elegant orchestral sound he successfully emulated, had divided up the lucrative field among themselves. Mendelssohn focused on the concert hall; Meyerbeer on the opera house. There seemed to be nothing left over for their young aspiring competitor.

---

[236] *Ibid.*, p. 32.
[237] *Ibid.*, p. 41.
[238] *Ibid.*, p. 36.
[239] *Ibid.*, p. 31.
[240] *Ibid.*, p. 47.

All the same, they did not treat Wagner badly. Meyerbeer even supported him, and Mendelssohn Bartholdy characterized him (patronizingly, perhaps) as a "brilliant dilettante."[241] Neither ever acted hostilely, but rather treated him with the courteous indifference normal among competitive colleagues. Wagner, though, experienced this as insulting nonchalance, which left him squeezed, while they themselves enlisted press and public to boost their own celebrity, and were in the process—as he was firmly convinced—working to his detriment.

We can now actually observe the curious phenomenon that from his earliest appearance, Wagner met with a wave of derision that regarded him in effect as unworthy of serious criticism. When the little man was surprisingly named to the position of Court Kapellmeister following his *Rienzi* triumph, and sought at once to bring to that office new, revolutionary importance, he was given the demeaning nick-name "Tinsmith" by an influential privy councilor,[242] which soon evolved further into "Tiny Tin-pot Potentate."[243] "The Ninth Symphony—what would it be without him?" asked a mocking detractor, and added maliciously, "O let us draw his carriage in triumph, and kneel before the great genius of our time and of posterity."[244]

Of course this was all in good fun, and everyone knew that his friend Karl Gutzkow was behind it. But for Wagner this satirical verse was a further humiliation, which undermined his reputation in the city. The initial

---

[241] *Ibid.*, p. 32.
[242] *Ibid.*, p. 24.
[243] "Kleiner Blechkönig."
[244] Glasenapp, v. II, p. 302.

reviews had already struck this facetious tone. He was not welcomed as a new composer, but rather as the butt of peculiar jokes, as a comical figure and laughing stock, whose rebuff in the daily press would see to it — and see to it for some time to come — that performance of his works would appear utterly gratuitous.

Who would want anything to do with a composer of whom Heinrich Dorn, for example, said he regarded "every piece of his own excrement the effluent of divine inspiration?"[245] The dismissal of these "effluents" from Wagner's supposedly delirious brain followed soon after. It was always the same names wielding ever the same wisecracks that were responsible for relegating Wagner's creations to the realm of cheap imitation, amateurish craftsmanship, ludicrous conceit, and even madness. That these highly imaginative articles incidentally took their toll on business was entirely intentional on the part of their authors.

In 1843, an invitation went out to all the men's choral societies in Saxony to a mass festival of art song, and the Court Kapellmeister was commissioned to write a "larger piece for male chorus," which — as he noted humorously in *Mein Leben* — "should most nearly fill out the time of half an hour."[246] This composition by stopwatch resulted in the oratorio for the Feast of Pentecost, *Das Liebesmahl der Apostel*, in whose score the critic Dr. Julius Schladebach — himself an amateur composer — spotted easy prey. Through this occasional work, which nonetheless received a successful performance in the Frauenkirche, Schladebach made the creator of *The Flying Dutchman* and *Rienzi* out to be a rank amateur, whose "inability to write in the rigorous style [is]

---

[245] Tappert, p. 31.
[246] Wagner, *Mein Leben*, p. 270.

everywhere admirably documented." Nevertheless, Wagner had known how to get himself "raised to the heavens [as the] passionately anticipated operatic Messiah."

Since this confidence man — in the words of the Dresden critic — possessed no "truly specific musical talent," he felt obliged to post a warning notice: "We cannot advise any society whose members are not willfully prepared to ruin voice, chest, and lungs to rehearse a Wagner composition." Risks and side-effects were also indicated, and not only with respect to the *Liebesmahl*, but to all other extant or future Wagnerian works. This verdict, approaching a performance ban, was published in the specialty journal for male choral singing *Teutonia*, whose editor (no surprise) was Dr. Julius Schladebach.[247]

Wagner for his part was marked for life by this experience. Even in old age, when an illustrated journal deferentially asked the famous man for his "memories," he had a friend reply on his behalf that "he had no memories at all except of bad newspaper reviews."[248]

That Meyerbeer and Mendelssohn should rise to Olympian heights, while he himself stumbled from one obstacle to the next fed his suspicion that he had to bear the professional costs of their praise — as his two competitors the financial. Heinrich Heine had already enlightened him on the reality that in Paris, artistic success was not achieved, but had to be purchased, and that anyone too poor to pay, would also remain poor. Wagner transferred this to the Dresden situation, believing he recognized the same mechanism at work.

---

[247] Glasenapp, v. II, p. 527.
[248] Cosima Wagner, *Diaries*, April 5, 1878.

The two favorites, who, to add insult to injury were of Jewish extraction, greased the palms of opera directors, press, and claque in order to sweep all competition—of his caliber particularly—out of the way. Because these machinations by their very nature occurred "under the table," Wagner, who felt victimized by a hypocritical mafia, struck a sarcastic and insinuating tone, whose venomous humor he hoped would compensate all the mischief done him. The result: his awful essay *Judaism in Musik*, in which Wagner calls for its "downfall,"[249] all the while actually meaning Meyerbeer and Mendelssohn.

Nor did his opponents, whose number was multiplied by his anti-Semitic derailing, leave it at jokes, satire, and deeper meaning. By Wagner's account, his acquaintance of many years, the poet Heinrich Laube, let the composer know, "that he could never have imagined so desperate a situation as that in which I found myself in opposition to the whole of journalism, and when he learned my view of the matter, smiling, he gave me his blessing as quite simply a lost man."[250] The "view" alluded to was essentially Wagner's life-long courageous as well as fateful habit of not only *not* courting reviewers and other influential opinion makers—as they considered their due—but actually snubbing them as often as possible. Aside from the art of turning friends into creditors, he had mastered also

---

[249] "*Untergang*,," literally "going under." The ambiguity of the German word has led to much scholarly debate over Wagner's usage in this notorious essay. Its meanings are various, as given in *Langenscheidt's Encyclopedic Muret-Sanders German Dictionary*, (Berlin & Munich, 1975): viz., setting (of the sun), sinking (of a ship), shipwreck, downfall, decline, eclipse, destruction, extinction, ruin. Usage thus ranges from the topographic to the apocalyptic.
[250] Wagner, *Mein Leben*, p. 263.

the art of turning friends into enemies. That may be the reason his dramas teem with "quite simply lost men."

Venomous Humor. Portrait by the Viennese costume designer Franz Gaul. Wagner, as polemical writer with sharpened pen, presented caricaturists an easy target.

The attitude reigning in Bayreuth that it was besieged by legions of hostile pens was not created entirely out of thin air. During construction of the festival theater, the *Frankfurter Zeitung* in 1874 ran the writer Kastan's unvarnished assessment that "Wagner does not fall into the classification of the unsound of mind one shuts up in madhouses, or places under police surveillance. He belongs rather to those one must fight to the point of annihilation."[251]

In London in 1855 Wagner might experience just that. Invited to conduct a series of concerts, his visit was heralded by a reputation that made it appear inadvisable for any serious music lover to grace his performances with their attendance. As though to confirm his arguably paranoid suspicion of having been placed on a black list, the local critics praised his competitors as decisively as they warned against him as though he constituted a morally corrupting public menace—which, as we have seen, did not prevent the Queen from showing him the honor of her small talk.

One of the two London anti-Wagnerians, Henry F. Chorley, incidentally, is imortalized in the history of press canards for having written a glowing obituary of Ivan Turgenev . . . while the latter was still living. It was otherwise in the Case of Wagner, whom Chorley planned to bury even before his arrival in London. In the invitation to the German itself, Chorley saw "nothing short of a wholesale offence to the native and foreign conductors resident in England."[252] Since the creator of *The Flying Dutchman*, *Tannhäuser*, and *Lohengrin* produced "noise, strictly speaking--not

---

[251] Tappert, p. 123.
[252] Ernest Newman, *Richard Wagner*, (New York, 1937), v. II., p. 465.

music,"[253] and altogether sparkled with "perversity and poverty in special gifts combined,"[254] Chorley's "most strenuous critical efforts of this period were made . . . to withstand the attempts of the modern German schools, represented by Schumann and Herr Wagner, to obtain a permanent footing" in England.[255]

For England had no need of him—she already had Mendelssohn and Meyerbeer. While Chorley, critic for *Atheneum*, stressed the "delicious impression" Meyerbeer's music first made on him,[256] he contrasted Wagner's orchestral sound, inappropriate because "strident," to "the full, brilliant, well-nourished sound (to adopt the French phrase), . . . we find in Mendelssohn's *tenor* orchestra . . ."[257] The fronts, then, were established before Wagner had yet mounted the podium, and the damning reviews, so it seems, written before he had even put down his baton.

Thanks to pronounced self-irony, in the long run the composer so defamed was able to set aside these sorts of low blows from the media. That mixed into every success was the bitter pill of failure, and conversely that each defeat might turn around into an astonishing resurrection, was simply a fundamental, annoying aspect of his life. While the London audience applauded him enthusiastically as the London press was tearing him down, he wrote home to Zürich about the Queen's red nose and the conversations they no doubt had concerning Peps and Papo. At the same time he worked undeterred on the second part of *The Ring of*

---

[253] Henry F. Chorley, *Modern German Music*, (London, 1854), p. 348.
[254] *Ibid.*, p. 369.
[255] Henry F. Chorley, *Autobiography, Memoirs and Letters*, (London, 1873), v. II, pp. 192-93.
[256] Chorley, *Modern German Music*, p. 365.
[257] *Ibid.*, p. 366.

the Nibelung, The Valkyrie, whose first act he completed in London. It was no coincidence that the London Wagner resembled his hero, the hunted outlaw Siegmund, who defies an overwhelming foe, though in vain, as the laws of tragedy decree.

As Wagner's irrepressible humor again would have it, he saw in the doomed figure of Siegmund a "Germanic Don Quixote,"[258] that is, the idealist foundering tragically on reality, and in one and the same person the risible "Knight of the Sorrowful Countenance," who takes windmills for giants and a coarse country girl for Princess Dulcinea. It was not just in the figure of Siegmund that Wagner carried out this secret identification with the kindly-comic daydreamer, but also precisely in those of his protagonists of whom we would least expect it. "Don Quixote," he once remarked to Cosima, was "actually an avatar of the Grail Knight,"[259] which throws an unfamiliarly profane, even humorous light on Wagner's miracle-working luminous heroes, Lohengrin and Parsifal — illumination mixed of victory's glory and the gloom of candle-glow ... with which their creator was all too familiar.

Scene 2

When Tannhäuser Wed Elisabeth

Comedy was everywhere, if mostly hidden. Each of his works was wreathed about with commentaries, jeers, and observations — sometimes coming from himself, sometimes from his admirers or detractors — that seem on the surface scarcely to touch on the deep, often

---

[258] Glasenapp, v. VI, p. 276.
[259] Cosima Wagner, *Diaries*, August 4, 1878.

sacramental seriousness of his dramas. In truth, though, they form the historical key without which the message in its existential urgency cannot be understood at all. Only through the frivolity "at the periphery" is the metaphysical kernel, immune to mockery, openly revealed. Absent the satyr play with its dancing clowns, the tragedy of death and transfiguration lapses into ritual, tucked safely away in the repertoire drawer.

Wagner danced with them. None of his works were spared his satire. It was surely with eyebrows raised in astonishment that Cosima recorded in her diaries his jokes about Bayreuth and the family treasure. His partisan Ludwig Schemann also reported that the Master "more often jokingly, less frequently seriously, discussed his own works,"[260] not because he had any doubts about his dramas, but because their reception formed so grotesque a contrast to his expectations. Instead of being understood as philosophical-artistic revelations, they were either worshipped blindly, or consumed as ordinary (if somewhat tedious) costume dramas, since a body of spiteful criticism had already dismissed them as sub-par hackwork.

Recalling *Rienzi*—satirized as "Meyerbeer's best opera"— which does not number among the "Seven Wonders of the World," Wagner described this contrast between intention and reception, which for once at least had the laughers on his side. In one of the few scenes in *Mein Leben* in which his older brother Julius, goldsmith and black sheep of the family, makes an appearance, Wagner reveals for his readers the "truly thrilling moment of this opera." In a Leipzig performance of *Rienzi*, to which he had taken his brother, naturally all

---

[260] Schemann, p. 53.

eyes were on Wagner's box. To forestall unnecessary gossip, the composer writes, "I forbade him from any expression of approval, even if only with respect to the singers." And in fact, Julius managed to refrain from applauding throughout the evening. Only at a particular point in the ballet did his enthusiasm get the better of him such that, in response to the cheers of the audience he madly beat his hands together, and indicated to me that he was now unable to hold back any longer."

Julius's enthusiasm for the ballet was not a unique case. "Remarkably," Wagner wrote, "my *Rienzi*, otherwise indifferently received, owed its continuing partiality on the part of the current King of Prussia to just this ballet, even though it was utterly unable to warm the audience with its dramatic content." When *Rienzi* was given in Darmstadt, Wagner discovered that the "best parts" of his dramatic composition had been cut, whereas the balletic interpolations had been significantly expanded. The highpoint was reached when an entire company of soldiers marched in, their "shields held touching each other above their heads to form a roof," so that "the ballet master and his assistant, dressed in flesh-colored tights," could perform head-stands on them. "This was the moment that always electrified the house into resounding applause, and I had to tell myself when this moment arrived that I had attained the pinnacle of my success."[261]

The fact that with *The Flying Dutchman*, which followed *Rienzi* in 1843, the era of the truly Wagnerian opera had begun left his laughing critics unimpressed. They were not prepared to concede that someone regarded as a

---

[261] Wagner, *Mein Leben*, p. 257.

127

con-man, or at least labelled one, should suddenly come forth with something astonishingly new. If a "wonder work" be defined as not confining itself merely to presenting something new in a pre-existing space, rather on the contrary opening up an entirely new space for it to inhabit, then this applied to *The Flying Dutchman*—as do Wagner's following six stage works (counting *The Ring* as a single work). Each opened new horizons and presented a new tonal language to unlock for the audience a hitherto unknown world of sound and idea. His admirers sank on their knees before these true wonders; his detractors clung to their established picture of Wagner. Anything bearing the name "Wagner" was filled with the ridiculous; until, upping the ante, they began to find the downright "immoral" in it. The wonder world he set before the eyes and ears of his audience, they were blind to, were resolved to remain blind to, and dismissed altogether as "monkey theater."

The caterwaul came from both sides. To Wagner's great disappointment, his new "music drama" was unable to ride the success of *Rienzi* because *The Flying Dutchman* dared to break with the beloved tradition of the Meyerbeeresque costume drama. No crowds in parti-colored garments marching across an immense stage, singing and waving flags. Instead, the entire action, from the howl of the storm and the roar of the waves, to the wail of the chorus of spirits, occurred actually in the music. Against that background, no historical spectacle played out—only the dark drama of love and suicide of two "lost souls."

"My process was new,"[262] Wagner explained. The story, though, was not. He had come across the wittily recounted sea-farer's fable among Heinrich Heine's writings, whose undertone of irony he had disapproved, for in Paris his stock of "all irony" and "all bitter or humorous sarcasm" had been depleted.[263] So he restored Heine's frivolous legend to the mythical-elemental dimension, divesting the horror of Weber's wolf's glen of its childish details—recall little Richard's *papier-mache* boar on rollers—and loosed it on the audience as it were in its undiluted form. That a genteel orchestra should here be rendering acoustically the eeriness of the destructive forces of nature provoked condescending laughter among the critics. Theatrical immediacy was scorned as ignorance of the rules; tamelessness, as want of grace. The aforementioned London critic Henry F. Chorley, for example, could not resist the impression of "grim violence and dreary vagueness," and indeed positively collapsed under this assault, "which till then at least had never been produced in such a fullness of ugliness by the music of a clever man."[264]

The public, which thanks to the press was *au courant* about the new "Kapellmeister Kreisler," received *The Flying Dutchman* unenthusiastically—felt rather, in Wagner's formulation, "all the less moved to demonstrations of approval, as the genre itself annoyed them."[265] Soon he was filled with unhappy certainty "that I had not hereby pleased the Dresden audience."[266] It went no better for him with the Berlin

---

[262] Glasenapp, *Wagner-Enzyklopädie*, v. I, p. 280.
[263] Ibid., p. 278.
[264] Chorley, *Modern German Music*, p. 352.
[265] Glasenapp, *Wagner-Enzyklopädie*, v. I, p. 284.
[266] Wagner, *Mein Leben*, p. 255.

production, cancelled despite its promising adoption into the repertoire because the management, as Wagner noted, had been governed by "a sure instinct for the state of the modern theater,"[267] which was dominated by names—he was convinced—among which his was not to be found because he did not pony up.

He was most annoyed by the very loose way his score was handled in Mannheim—though he could also see a comical side to the experience. As he quickly noted on a visit to the performance, his death-enthralled Dutchman had been bereft, by radical "prank surgery," of characteristic aspects of his scene, whereas a rather unassuming duet had been presented to its broadest imaginable extent. "A tenor, whose misfortune it was to sow fatigue the moment he made an entrance, had apparently insisted on the undiminished performance of his role, while the conductor apparently took his revenge by stretching out the tempo of Erik's passionate lover's plaint with quarters beaten regularly at a truly torturous pace." For good measure, "the Herr Kapellmeister arrogantly executed the office of censor and cut the final act, merely because he found it personally annoying."[268]

Wagner's frustration over the mistreatment of his circumnavigating sailor, in which audience, management, and critics shared equally, weighed the more heavily because the composer identified with the Dutchman—in a strictly humorous way, of course. The perpetually despairing one, who like Addison's Cato could hardly expect the all-destroying "annihilating blow," he described with irony as "my vigorously

---

[267] Glasenapp, *Wagner-Enzyklopädie*, v. I, p. 284.
[268] *Ibid.*, p. 285.

The Laughing Wagner

suffering, terrible sea-farer,"[269] whose "difficult role" it was "to evoke profoundest sympathy."[270]

Wagner claimed this for himself as well. Plowing through his ontological ocean restlessly and aimlessly, and hoping vainly for warm sympathy, he saw himself in the maritime man of sorrows, only just a notch higher. "The Flying Dutchman is nothing compared to me,"[271] he said jokingly to Cosima. And elsewhere, referring to his own fate, he quoted the sea-farer's lofty paradox: "Bereft of hope as I am, I devote myself all the same to hope!"[272]

The Dutchman soon found fellow sufferers. Hopelessly caught between lust and love, service to Venus and veneration of Saints, Wagner's next hero found himself in a similar dilemma, from which there was but one escape, the so-called "redemption." In *Tannhäuser* too, there is only the escape of *The Flying Dutchman*, in which the enamored protagonists do not reach the conclusion of the opera alive. "With this work, I wrote my own death sentence," Wagner noted half resigned, half amused. "Facing the modern world of art, I could no longer now hope for life."[273]

Truly, with Tannhäuser, he had succeeded in a further revolution in the genre of traditional opera, for which its defenders could not forgive him. Since they controlled the theater box offices, they drove this eccentric "upstart" into a corner like a freak to be

---

[269] Wagner, *Mein Leben*, p. 255.
[270] Glasenapp, *Wagner-Enzyklopädie*, v. I, p.282.
[271] Cosima Wagner, *Diaries*, July 18, 1871.
[272] *Richard Wagner an seine Künstler, Zweiter Band der "Bayreuther Briefe,"* Herausgegeben von Erich Kloss, dritte Auflage, (Leipzig, 1912), p. 377.
[273] Glasenapp, *Wagner-Enzyklopädie*, v. 2, p. 214.

gawked at, who could keep his head above water only by incurring further debt. James Davison, the powerful critic of *The Times*, tore Wagner's work to pieces. He boldly declared that "a more bombastic expenditure of incongruity and noise has seldom been offered the public," and warned Londoners that "even the most wonderful performance could not make this 'Tannhäuser' music acceptable, and we hope with all our hearts that no performance, however marvelous, should ever lead to the situation that such meaningless discords should in England be held to demonstrate they have anything in common with art or genius."[274]

Davison's German colleagues likewise shook their heads and sharpened their pens. In a guide book to Dresden, Wagner might read about the "musical worthlessness" of his "most vulgarly lascivious"[275] music, and in Germany's leading critical periodical, Robert Schumann's *Neue Zeitschrift für Musik*, he could even witness his own execution spread leisurely across two issues, and thus drawn-out over a long (though entertaining, in light of the reviewer's jests) period of time.

An example: as high- and end-point of the Venusberg scene, Wagner's hero is transported into a kind of religious ecstasy, in which, in the very heart of the "cave of lust,"[276] he prays to the Mother of God for salvation from the snares of the love goddess. "All the preceding," Wagner wrote, had been only "a powerful heightening of the crucial cry, 'My salvation rests with Maria!'" which must come with such force "that the immediately occurring miracle of the disenchantment

---

[274] Glasenapp, v. III, p. 98.
[275] Tappert, p. 68.
[276] Glasenapp, *Wagner-Enzyklopädie*, v. I, p. 348.

The Laughing Wagner

of the Venusberg . . . is quickly grasped" by the audience. The critic, on the other hand, could make no sense—he was joking, of course—of Tannhäuser's fervent prayer. "In order to free himself from Venus's power, he says, 'My salvation rests with Maria!' Reflexively, one reaches for one's program to learn who this 'Maria' might be."[277]

It is no coincidence that one may read in the writings of Nietzsche, Wagner's intimate, how to kill with laughter, and any victim of a scathing review knows how such reading feels. That Wagner, after the painful, drawn-out torment, did not hang up his profession—and himself with it—can again be explained only by his deeply ingrained humor and his equally deep-seated thirst for revenge, sinister twin of the need for recognition. Only a few years after his exposure to universal ridicule in the *Neue Zeitschrift für Musik*, in the same periodical, likewise anonymously and spread over two issues, he launched his "Judaism in Music," in which he treated those he held responsible for his own earlier disparagement to the same atrocious ridicule. One may easily judge from the tortured humor of his tirade how the *Tannhäuser* reviewer's humor had hit home.

At times, he simply laughed off his annoyance over bad reviews. Following the premiere performance of the *Tannhäuser* Overture in Paris in 1850—without success, needless to say—the rejected artist forwarded the review from a French newspaper to his friend Kietz. "To my greatest satisfaction," wrote a relaxed Wagner, "[I have come upon] the following brilliant observation about my Overture: This musical composition (I

---

[277] Glasenapp, v. II, p. 526.

translate accurately) contained the noisy accompaniment to an absent melody. In any case, Wagner understands much about harmony and instrumentation; unfortunately, heaven has stubbornly denied him the gift of melody. There are no laws against writing; certain laws in some countries forbid only certain ideas. Now, no country's laws will have anything to object to in the performance of Wagner's works, for these contain no ideas whatsoever."[278]

Though there are certainly things for which one could reproach Wagner, he was second to none when it came to original ideas. *Tannhäuser*, too, offers a pyrotechnic display of dramaturgical and musical ideas, which already in the opening scene, the plush rosy bower of the love-goddess, offer surprising highlights — for instance when the seductress implores her lover bluntly to perform his cavalier's duty, while he, overwhelmed by pangs of conscience, is craving the blessing of the holy Virgin.

Already at the premiere, this awkward coupling, not easily grasped, went seriously wrong. As in *Rienzi* and *The Flying Dutchman*, the leading role was taken by Wilhelmine Schröder-Devrient, whose Valkyrie-like figure had not — shall we say — ordained her for the role of love-goddess. Confronting the question of her costume, she groaned, "smiling desperately, 'For God's sake, what in the world should I wear as Venus? Just a girdle will never do!'"[279] Even "just a girdle" could not have solved the problem: Schröder-Devrient simply

---

[278] Wagner, *Sämtliche Briefe*, v. III, p. 480.
[279] Wagner, *Mein Leben*, p. 317.

lacked—in Wagner's discreet formulation—an "auspicious exterior configuration."[280]

The fact that the scene was completely "unsuccessful," actually "painful," though, was attributable rather to the hero. He was simply not equal to either the role or his leading lady. Though gifted with a brilliant voice, the renowned tenor Tichatschek could "not comprehend"[281] the part, and that because of a lack which Wagner, in his confident diagnosis, blamed on "the obstinacy of his character and the smallness of his brain."[282]

Tichatschek (known as "Tschekel") had mastered the role of the People's Tribune Rienzi brilliantly in his 400 Thaler silver armor, but the role of suffering troubadour was beyond him, so that the character's tragedy quite eluded the audience. For as little as Schröder-Devrient could credibly convey the power of her charms to enthrall a troubadour, Tschekel in the role of the great abstainer was just as incapable of convincing the audience that he would abandon an eagerly willing paramour to kneel before the image of a saint. In the hedonist Tschekel, whom Wagner jokingly called a "libertine and dissolute person,"[283] the audience simply could not imagine the figure of an ascetic and self-flagellator. So the misalliance in the Grotto of Venus was complete, and the premiere's failure sealed.

The disaster of the 1860 Paris production of *Tannhäuser*, whose direction had been assigned the composer, unfolded even more terribly. One bone of contention

---

[280] Glasenapp, *Wagner-Enzyklopädie*, v. II, p. 218.
[281] Ibid., v. II, p. 222.
[282] Wagner, *Sämtliche Briefe*, v. IV, p. 378.
[283] *Ibid.*, p. 228.

was the overly short balletic interpolations, which incensed the male audience members, obsessed as they were with skimpy tutus. A single ballet, appearing before the intermission supper at that, flew in the face of the Parisian concept of art. And it was not just the ticket-buyers whom the German rubbed the wrong way; he was also strongly at odds with the ballet master, who incidentally mocked Wagner's mode of locomotion by climbing over things.

Choreographer Lucien Petipa had no idea where to begin with Wagner's vision of the Grotto of Venus—the German was simply ahead of him by half a century. For the classical ballet master, dance consisted of a stationary, geometrically mapped-out sequence of movements, not so different from the drill of the *Grande Armée*, whereas Wagner saw in it the exact opposite: the dynamic expression of feelings and emotional relationships, in which the liberation of the human being from all artificial constraint broke new ground. But his attempt to persuade the choreographer that "the dance in the Venusberg is no dance in the manner conventional in our opera and ballet," but rather "a seductive, wild, and overwhelming chaos of groupings and movements, from the mildest bliss, yearning, and desire, to the most drunken exuberance of jubilant abandon,"[284] left the drill sergeant of the "rat"-corps cold.

When an irritated Wagner finally pointed out to Petipa "that the pitifully hopping little steps of his maenads and bacchants stood in rather silly contrast to my music," his interlocutor put on an ironic smile, whistled through his fingers like an animal trainer, "and said to

---

[284] Glasenapp, *Wagner-Enzyklopädie*, v. II, p. 219.

me: 'Were I to say a word of this to my people and let them know the tenor of your attitude, we would instantly have the Cancan, and all would be lost.'"[285] This misapprehension that equated liberation of the body with the popular dance cabaret portended the larger reality that Wagner's drama of the soul was to be judged by the standards of the Parisian spectacle. Here, the composer could only lose, and his poor troubadour, seeking redemption from this earthly vale of sorrows, went down in a hail of boos and cat-calls. Wagner's futile half-year in Paris garnered precisely 750 Francs, which completed the disaster.[286]

Although following the Dresden premiere Wagner's maid had assured him, "the people in her circle had found this opera 'even more beautiful than Rienzi,'"[287] he was virtually bombarded with helpful suggestions for improvement. These people were well-intentioned, and meant to put an end to the misery that darkened his life, so they put their own imaginations to work. First to be cited must be Minna, who already during the orchestral rehearsals singled out an error in instrumentation: she dearly missed "the trumpets and trombones that had always provided such bubbly cheerfulness in *Rienzi.*"[288] Wagner recorded this in his memoirs without comment, but obviously tongue in cheek. In the same place we have the testimony of the versifying Court Theater Director, Heinrich Laube, who must have found the *Tannhäuser* music acceptable; it was, however, as Wagner wrote, "my bad luck not to

---

[285] *Ibid.*, v. II, p. 220.
[286] Gregor-Dellin, p. 469.
[287] Glasenapp, v. III, p. 133.
[288] Wagner, *Mein Leben*, p. 318.

have engaged a skillful dramatist to write a proper libretto for my music."[289]

Actually, Laube found much to object to in the composition as well, among other things the Venusberg music, which—as he explained to the composer—was "much too difficult," because "what belonged there was enticing, seductive melody in the Italian manner." Wagner listened calmly, and to Laube's surprise even conceded that "Schröder-Devrient had already told him that."[290] Possibly, the disinclination of that sober lady flowed not solely from the ecstatic effusions in the Venusberg, but also from her general attitude which, to her inamorato Herr von Bock, she summed up in the words that to her, Wagner had "always been exceptionally uncongenial as a composer."[291]

Even the Russian anarchist Mikhail Bakunin, who instigated the 1849 Dresden revolution, had time enough to provide his comrade-in-arms Richard suggestions for artistic improvement. When after the revolution everything had been "burnt up," Bakunin explained to him, he would no longer "need so many instruments, and that will be very good!"[292] In any case, the revolutionary seems to have preferred choral interludes. When Wagner showed him his sketch for *Jesus of Nazareth*, Bakunin recommended "setting only one text: the tenor should sing, 'Off with his head!,' the soprano, 'hang him!,' and the bass, 'Fire, fire!'"[293]

---

[289] *Ibid.*, p. 241.
[290] Glasenapp, v. III, p. 339.
[291] Alexander von Wolzogen, *Wilhelmine Schröder-Devrient*, (Leipzig, 1863), p. 307.
[292] Cosima Wagner, *Diaries*, November 27, 1879.
[293] Wagner, *Mein Leben*, p. 400.

Another revolutionary prophet, August Röckel, did great service in the matter of Wagner's acceptance by the public. Together with the set-designer Heine, he mobilized the latter's public relations technique, for whose employment Wagner had reproached his competitors Mendelssohn and Meyerbeer: viz., an organized claque, whose task it was, by targeted "explosions of applause"(in Wagner's words), to bring the hidden beauties of the work out into the proper light. "It now transpired," he reported further, "that one strong burst of applause prompted in this way following the words of Wolfram—'An angel pleads for you at God's throne; he is heard; Heinrich, you are redeemed!'—seemed with a single stroke to have illumined the meaningful situation for the entire audience. In all subsequent performances this moment, entirely unremarked at the premiere, remained a principal spot for demonstration of approval by the audience."[294]

There was also much to complain about with respect to content. The event just described in the finale—a coffin with the newly expired virgin appears, whereupon the hero falls dead crying, "Holy Elisabeth, pray for me!"— seemed to Dresden Court Theater Director von Lüttichau (a former chief forester) all too agitating. As Wagner's superior, he proposed a more anodyne alternative: "let Tannhäuser find absolution in Rome and marry Elisabeth."[295]

What the court toady found too stimulating, appeared on the contrary all too dry to Karl Gutzkow. "Apart from the charming polonaise," remarked the poet who had also penned the hymn to the "Young Tin-pot

---

[294] *Ibid.*, p. 328.
[295] Cosima Wagner, *Diaries*, January 6, 1883.

Potentate," "Tannhäuser seemed tedious to me." He missed a touch of the satanic. "Why have you left Klingsohr out of your contest on the Wartburg?" he asked Wagner, alluding to the evil magician who supplies the tension in Hoffmann's singing contest, conjuring up that very spirit Nasias, whose name Wagner would years later give his nasal respirator.

That the composer might warm to his suggestion, Gutzkow referenced a Meyerbeer hit opera whose popularity Wagner could up to then only have dreamed of. "You would have achieved it," the poet advised him, "with a powerful bass role *à la* Bertram in *Robert le Diable*, and in the plot an agent of the demonic in dramatic form, who would act on Tannhäuser!"[296] It had eluded the jokester that in *Tannhäuser* none other than the titular hero himself is responsible for the "demonic in pleasure and pain."[297]

Gutzkow's bold suggestion for improvement fell nonetheless — if belatedly — on fertile ground. Decades later, the magician Klingsor turned up in the Bayreuth *Parsifal* as the satanic adversary of the titular hero. Incidentally, long before Wagner, the depressive Gutzkow had experienced life in that provincial Upper-Franconian town. He had committed himself for treatment for suicidal moods to a Bayreuth specialty clinic, where at times — as Wagner learned from a neighboring psychiatrist — he rose to become the "glory of the madhouse."[298]

---

[296] Barth/Mack/Voss, p. 311.
[297] Glasenapp, *Wagner-Enzyklopädie*, v. II, p. 226.
[298] Cosima Wagner, *Diaries*, June 1, 1872. Dr. Falko's asylum was so near the Festival Theater, they actually were neighbors. The joke among "anti-Wagnerians" was that the Master would make the perfect patient. On a walk in this area once, Nietzsche lost his way and asked at the asylum for directions home.

The Laughing Wagner

Another poet, the humorist Johann Nestroy, was moved to make suggestions for improvement to *Tannhäuser*. In his parody of the same name, premiered in Vienna in 1857, he succumbed to the same idea as Gutzkow, of marrying off the tragic lovers at the end. So as not to forgo the effect of their double death, Nestroy, to the delight of the audience, invested the scantily clad love goddess with the power to reawaken the unhappily deceased lovers to life:

> *"Bonjour, Messieurs, I am the goddess of love*
> *And graciously draw near this bed of sorrows.*
> *The love of this maiden moves me deeply,*
> *And truly, I am not jealous, not one bit:*
> *May they awaken, to delight in each other*
> *And resume the course of their love.*
> *This one condition, though, is my commandment:*
> *At the first quarrel, you instantly are dead again!"*[299]

Nestroy's Wagner parody became an acclaimed, long-running hit, and even the satire's target himself did not pass up the opportunity of attending a performance. As his disciple Peter Cornelius reported, it apparently "put [him] in the most cheerful of moods."[300]

A psychiatrist invited him in, where one of the patients gave him a poem, titled "*Christus als Schmetterlingsrüssel*" ("Christ as Proboscis of a Butterfly"). Wagner was highly amused.

[299] *Richard der Einzige*. Hermann Hakel, ed., (Vienna, 1963), p. 98. "Bonjour, Messieurs, ich bin der Liebe Göttin/Und trete gnädig an dies Trau'rbett hin./Die Liebe dieses Fräuleins rührt mich tüchtig,/Und ich bin wirklich gar nicht eifersüchtig:/Erwachen mögen sie, sich zu ergötzen/Und ihre Liebe wieder fortzusetzen./Doch die Bedingung sprech ich als Gebot:/Beim ersten Streit seid ihr gleich wieder tot!"

[300] Cornelius, v. I, p. 403.

Scene 3

Watermusic for Fifty Spiked Helmets

Nestroy's astonishing success with the *Tannhäuser* parody, fueled in no small part by *Schadenfreude*, encouraged the comic writer in due course to pick apart Wagner's next opera, *Lohengrin*. In Nestroy's version, the Swan Knight appears *sans* boat, nor is he drawn by a swan, rather by a sheep hitched to the hero's wagon. His melancholy words of farewell on Wagner's melody triggered veritable storms of applause:

> "Now be thanked, my loyal sheep,
> Go home again to magical sleep,
> Be nicely patient, kind, and good,
> Such as I've truly never seen a sheep be;
> Farewell, Farewell, my loyal sheep!"[301]

But nonsense-rhymes numbered also—like those cited above on Heine's "May" poem—among Wagner's special talents. Anyone who finds his alliterative verse risible, should first read his satirical poems inspired by every imaginable occasion. "Tschekel" Tichatscheck, whose "good-natured sheep's aspect"[302] Wagner found worth mentioning, enjoyed the roles and costumes of the Grail Knights, and wanted to perform them on the Rostock stage. The difficulty was that the Rostock Director, a certain Hugo Hünerfürst, feared he "would suffer excessively"[303] from Wagner's financial demands. The tenor pleaded with the composer for a discounted

---

[301] *Richard der Einzige*, p. 108. "Nun sei bedankt, mein gutes Schaf,/Kehr wieder heim zum Zauberschlaf,/Sei fein geduldig, lieb und brav,/Wie ich fürwahr kein Schaf noch traf;/Leb wohl, leb wohl, mein gutes Schaf!"
[302] Wagner, *Sämtliche Briefe*, v. IV, p. 377.
[303] Glasenapp, v. III, p. 434.

fee for Hünerfest, whereupon he received the following reply, worthy of a Nestroy, from Wagner:

"To the Prince of hen and rooster,
the knight of most noble singing swans
I offer up the stuff of Lohengrin
for performance there at Rostock.
Not exactly coddled in the fee,
a poor devil ever and forever more,
to Germany's honor let me be paid,
whatever has not been squandered on the sets . . ."[304]

It was not just financially that *Lohengrin* required cutbacks, however. Today's most frequently mounted Wagner opera, the singing Grail Knight—whom he himself satirized as "Lohengrün"[305] suffered from start-up difficulties. What proved an additional obstacle was the fact that the Royal-Saxon Court Kapellmeister suddenly appeared as a firebrand of the 1849 revolution. Of all things, at the moment his pious Grail- and Eucharist-Knight was to begin rehearsals in Dresden, Wagner was scheming rebellion in that very city. Director von Lüttichau, who had once lobbied for Tannhäuser's marriage, held fast to the monarchy and forbade the performance.

Not even the trial run, at which Wagner read his libretto to a select audience, ran smoothly. At restaurateur Engel's inn on Postplatz where the

---

[304] Wagner, *Sämtliche Schriften und Dichtungen*, v. XII, p. 367. The first line puns on the name of Theater Director, "Hünerfürst," which sounds like "Chicken Prince." *"Dem Fürst der Hühner und der Hähne,/dem Ritter edelster Singe-Schwäne/geb' ich als Rohstoff Lohengrin/zur Aufführung in Rostock hin./Nicht grad' verwöhnt mit Honorar,/ein armer Teufel immerdar,/zu Deutschlands Ehr' sei mir gezahlt,/was auf der Leinwand nicht vermalt."*

[305] Richard Fricke, *Bayreuth vor dreißig Jahren*, (Dresden, 1906), p. 55. Wagner's satirical title: *Lohengreen*.

composers Schumann and Hiller, the painter Schnorr von Carolsfeld and Pecht, as well as the architect Semper had gathered in 1845 as the illustrious "Monday Society," Wagner met with an audience that was difficult to size up. Finally Robert Schumann, who for the most part had sat mute in a corner, broke his silence, declaring it was "incomprehensible how this text was to be set to music." The libretto, he later wrote Mendelssohn, had delighted, to be sure, but "primarily the set designers." Mendelssohn's friend Ferdinand Hiller took a similar line when he maintained that "Wagner's talent as a musician [was] in no way [sufficient] for this material." "The beautiful verses surely long for another composer; a large ambition and an inadequate ability—that is the great chasm into which the Grail Knight will probably sink."[306]

What actually was to happen with the Grail Knight in the Swan boat was long in doubt. In connection with the 1847 *Rienzi* production in Berlin, Wagner lobbied desperately for the support of the art-promoting King of Prussia. He presented the new *Lohengrin* poem to various notable figures, who might make a recommendation to Friedrich Wilhelm IV. The romantic poet Ludwig Tieck found much that was successful, some things to criticize, but could hardly imagine how music was to be written to it, and ultimately gave him the friendly brush off.

He got a warmer reception from the singer Henriette Sontag, once admired of Goethe, Beethoven, and Weber. At least it appeared so initially to the composer, who hopefully presented her his Grail poem. "On my visit the following morning, at which she announced she would send me an invitation to an

---

[306] Glasenapp, v. II, p. 143.

evening's musical entertainment she was arranging at her home in honor of the Grand Duke of Mecklenburg-Strelitz, her fatherly patron, she also," in the ironic verbosity of Wagner's *Mein Leben*, "returned to me my manuscript of the *Lohengrin* poem with the assurance that it had appealed to her greatly, and that often during her reading she had 'seen the little elves and fairies dancing before her eyes.'"[307]

"*Infernal Racket.*"   Wagner's patron Franz Liszt earned precious little applause for his efforts on behalf of his protégé's works. This caricature from the *Vienna Humor Pages* of 1876 shows him playing a "compositional steam engine," out of which Wagner's vaporous spirit rises.

---

[307] Wagner, *Mein Leben*, p. 363.

Wagner felt as though "cold water" had been "poured on him." *Lohengrin* was populated neither with fairies nor with elves, and aside from the enchanted swan, no other beings from the world of fairy tales appeared in it. It was possible that Sontag, as he believed, had not read the libretto at all, and was leading him by the nose. She may also have been suggesting something she could not tell him openly: though "little elves and fairies" made no appearance in *Lohengrin*, they were certainly part of the picture in Mendelssohn's *Midsummer Night's Dream*. Was Mme. Sontag perhaps trying to signal to him that her affections already lodged elsewhere, and that thus she could not offer the recommendation he was looking for? In the event, the Prussian Monarch gave him the cold shoulder.

In compensation, Wagner soon enjoyed the sponsorship of the anti-monarchist Mikhail Bakunin. Their historic alliance led not only to the failed Dresden Revolution of 1849, but also to Wagner's not having the opportunity to hear his *Lohengrin* for a long time. In Dresden, the opera was banned along with its composer, for whom a wanted poster was issued throughout German lands. He could only enjoy the Weimar premiere vicariously in Zürich, with the score on his lap and a pocket watch in his hand. Even eleven years later, he complained to the composer of the ill-fated *Les Troyens*, Hector Berlioz, that he "was the only German who had not yet heard my opera." Berlioz replied drily, "And I am the only Frenchman who has heard my opera!"[308]

Although the already legendary Franz Liszt had conducted the premiere of *Lohengrin* in Weimar, Wagner's success remained modest. For even "those who love him" had, after dutifully attending,

---

[308] Paul Lindau, *Nur Erinnerungen*, (Stuttgart, 1916), v. I., p. 73.

afterwards broadcast their biting commentaries. So, in a Hamburg music journal for instance, one might read that Wagner had also "in this work (not to mention his previous works) shown himself utterly unmusical. He had offered not music, just noise, indeed so dreadful all that was missing from the infernal racket onstage was cannon-fire."[309]

Even without cannons, the so-called *Lohengrin* racket proved successful on international stages. At rehearsals for the Vienna production of 1875 Wagner showed how much he identified with his heroic couple. First, he portrayed the Swan Knight, who, defying the "amazement of the masses, the venomous effusion of envy " like his creator, could not appear other than wonderful to his contemporaries.[310] Truly wondrous in fact appeared that which the nimble Wagner acted out on the Vienna rehearsal stage, where he demonstrated to the performers "every step and movement." As the opera impresario Angelo Neumann noted, when he finally "donned Lohengrin's helmet and seized his sword and shield to attack Telramund, we were initially overcome by a certain amusement. That soon gave way, however, to the greatest wonder and amazement at the agility and skill with which he carried out the battle, as though he had never had anything other than a sword and shield in his hands."

After Lohengrin, came his bride's turn. The 62-year-old Master of Bayreuth stepped forth as the tender maiden Elsa of Brabant "solemnly, both arms raised high, palms toward the audience, with transfigured features, gleaming eyes, gazing intently upwards, without so

---

[309] Barth/Mack/Voss, p. 336.
[310] Glasenapp, *Wagner Enzyklopädie*, v. I, p. 349.

much as a glance at the steps, descending them confidently, leaving a small space behind him for the train- and cloak-bearing pages."[311]

Even before the Swan Knight and his wingéd words of parting "My beloved swan" had conquered opera stages, military bands had discovered *Lohengrin* and incorporated it into their brassy repertoire. "Occasionally I encountered," Wagner remarked on one occasion, "the very friendly honor of being greeted by military bands playing excerpts from my operas."[312] Mostly, this occurred in connection with the unavoidable welcoming and birthday serenades, in which generous use of fanfares with kettle drum and cymbal crash was made.

This very friendly honor, which pursued him everywhere, could only have been a considerable burden, particularly when the pleasure of unexpectedly hearing his own musical themes was clouded by frustration at their being played incorrectly. In the late 1850's, when he withdrew from the stressful *ménage à trois* with Mathilde and Minna to Venice, then under the control of Austria, to work on the composition of *Tristan*, it "was unavoidable to come into contact with the local military band leaders," specifically on the Piazza San Marco, which he frequented to take his coffee. Three uniformed bands competed in alternation for the public's approval, and the composer could flatter himself that marches from *Lohengrin*, *Rienzi*, and *Tannhäuser* were performed to great applause.

It was not, however, pleasing to him. One evening, he heard from one of the uniformed conductors "the

---

[311] Neumann, p. 11.
[312] Glasenapp, *Wagner-Enzyklopädie*, v. I, p. 357.

Tannhäuser March, and I was annoyed by the sluggish tempo." After Wagner had let that be known, the delighted conducting officer invited him to a rehearsal, where the composer was given the opportunity of unburdening himself of his objections, which went "really quite well . . . contrary to all expectation." Encouraged by Wagner's generosity, on another occasion a second military band leader approached him, a member of the Austrian Navy, and expressed most humbly the wish to perform the *Rienzi* overture according to the composer's instructions. "What choice did I have? I had to go to the navy barracks, where a full-scale reception had been prepared for me, all the officers *en masse*, with all the formalities. The overture" (which he heard sitting at a restaurant table where he was just capping off his dessert with a "half-bottle of Champagne") "went very well." The following day — as was to be expected — "the conductor of the Hungarian Regiment presented himself, with pieces from *Lohengrin*."[313]

As little as such performances had to offer in artistic terms, Wagner always set great store by correct tempi, and did not hesitate to insist on them. During his final stay in Venice in 1883, on the Piazza San Marco he heard a *Lohengrin* in the style of a military band which did not please him at all. His annoyance over this, as well as over certain medical prohibitions that seemed pointless to him — "that he make no sudden movements," for instance — led to one of his seizures, during which he turned blue, and with his arms flailing, lost consciousness. When he had come to himself again, he let the conductor know he would like him to call in the evening at the Palazzo Vendramin,

---

[313] Wagner, *Sämtliche Briefe*, v. X, p. 119.

"that he might instruct him about the manifold incorrect tempi he had taken in the *Lohengrin* excerpts, because it was painful to hear them so badly distorted at these performances."[314]

Nonetheless Wagner does seem to have found a certain charm in these musical/military tributes, if only on account of the amusing contrast between such bombastic brass music and his impressionistic orchestral finesse. In connection with an evening banquet thrown for him at the Hotel Prince Karl in Darmstadt in 1872, the composer — whose "icy-grey" hair was tinged, "doubtless in consequence of artificial coloring, somewhat in the greenish" range — was offered by the President of the Wagner Society (a certain Captain Zeroni) the usual encomium. He was most fascinated — as he told another Society President — by the speaker's name. "Zeroni shall live," he wrote to Emil Heckel, "if only for the sake of his beautiful name! Yes, if we had such names, right? But, 'Wagner,' 'Heckel' — insufferable!"[315]

The man with the beautiful name crowned his tribute by bestowing an "enormous laurel wreath" around the neck of the astonished Wagner. The honoree, who placed little value on such greenery, had just begun his obligatory statement of thanks, when outside, despite a November downpour, the "military musicians of the Guard Regiment" took up their positions. Although their uniforms were already drenched, and water poured down over their spiked helmets, the more than fifty instrumentalists took up their disciplined march

---

[314] Glasenapp, v. VI, p. 718.
[315] Richard Wagner, *Bayreuther Briefe (1871-1883)*, (Leipzig, 1907), p. 63.

with drums, tympani, trombones, and trumpets, their music resounding even inside the banquet hall.

That the military band's enthusiasm for Wagner failed to be satisfactorily conveyed can perhaps be blamed on the approaching storm that extinguished the hurricane lamps lighting their music. "Under such deteriorating conditions," the Secretary of the Darmstadt Court Theater, Ludwig Winter, recalled, they skipped the *Tannhäuser* Overture, so that the siren song of Venus now assumed particular weight. Unfortunately, the transcription had been clumsy, for the cry of desire "Come my beloved! See the grotto there," ordinarily scored for the yearning *piano* of a clarinet, was "here performed by a blaring trumpet in a quite splendid *fortissimo*."[316] As high-point of the military serenade, the bridal chorus from *Lohengrin* followed, customarily played only at weddings, but which nonetheless — according to Cosima's diary — prompted a "very enthusiastic mood" in the banquet hall within.[317]

The honoree meanwhile, sat with the laurel wreath around his neck, "totally impassive, listening calmly." Following the roundly-applauded finale of this "water music," its purveyor, Military Kapellmeister Theodor Adam, in his dripping gala uniform, hand on his spiked helmet, stepped before the Master to receive his thanks. Not hesitating for a second, Wagner jumped to his feet, and unburdened himself of the gigantic laurel wreath by bestowing it around the neck of the nonplussed conductor.[318]

---

[316] Otto, p. 482.
[317] Cosima Wagner, *Diaries*, November 20, 1872.
[318] Otto, p. 482.

Wagner's frustration over his misunderstood "World Wonders" derived not only from the denseness of performers and their audiences, the fear of innovation of the theater directors, and the pleasure critics took in mockery. The publisher of his first three works already saw to it that the composer would reap no pleasure from his works. In Wagner's estimation, he was one of the embodiments of the "most peculiar, almost demonic misfortune,"[319] which seemed to pursue him throughout his life. The publisher was Carl Friedrich Meser; he held the rights to *Rienzi*, *The Flying Dutchman*, and *Tannhäuser*, and contrived to transform the contract of commission agreed to with Wagner in 1844 into an instrument of torture, that moreover entailed the composer in mountainous debt. "Of all the music dealers in the world," Wagner complained, "he just happens to be the most incompetent for such a business; and were one to distill the most pusillanimous, most unstable, and cowardly Philistine down to his very essence, then it is just this Meser who would be the result. This person tormented me relentlessly during my last years in Dresden. I can say that a great measure of all the martyrdom I have ever suffered is named 'Meser.'"[320]

This secret misery was not hidden from the critics, and the amusing story of the unfortunate music dealer whose torments were all presumably marked with the name "Wagner" made its way as far as Vienna. In 1847, while he was working on *Lohengrin*, the *Wiener Musikzeitung* reported direct from Dresden that a "composing Kapellmeister" (in whom Wagner could easily be recognized) had driven his "music dealer"

---

[319] Glasenapp, v. III, p. 429.
[320] Wagner, *Sämtliche Briefe*, v. IV, p. 110.

into social decline, which was depicted in the ascent through the various floors of an apartment building. If Meser had formerly occupied the *"bel-étage,"* in the wake of Wagner's first opera, he had to move a floor higher. The second opera of the prolific composer drove the publisher up yet another floor, and the third opera another, so that he now lived four floors up, and was compelled to reject the fourth opera or end up in the attic."[321]

The rule according to which for Wagner harm and mockery always appeared together was confirmed in the case of that "fourth opera," *Lohengrin*, which though he could not hear the work itself, its scathing reviews were delivered gratis to his door. For his part, Meser was spared the indignity of moving to the garret on the Grail Knight's account: in 1850, the year of the *Lohengrin* premiere, Wagner's tormenting spirit died, perhaps because he could not get over the composer's financial misfortune.

As is well known, it took another fifteen years before the next Wagner opera saw its premiere. In the case of *Tristan und Isolde*, it was no longer a matter of an "opera," because in the meantime Wagner had distanced himself from this "decadent" métier, and devoted himself entirely to the "music drama." In his essay in aesthetic theory "Opera and Drama" (a tough nut to crack for the less philosophically inclined), he lays a persuasive foundation for this choice. From *Tristan* onwards, then, there were no further Wagner "operas"; the term itself was forbidden at Bayreuth.

---

[321] Glasenapp, v. II, p. 254.

Wagner called the new work—simple and striking in the truest sense—a "treatment."[322]

Scene 4

Liebestod and Schadenfreude

One needn't be a dyed-in-the-wool Wagnerite to know that *Tristan* represents a special case. Even those who find the designation "the Seven Wonders of the World" hard to swallow as applied to Wagner might concede its aptness to this work at least. Nietzsche, the initially intoxicated, then disillusioned Bayreuth apostle, called *Tristan* an *"opus metaphysicum,"* suggesting it has transcended the realm of the artistic-representational into the ether of sacred veneration.

In truth, everything in this opera—no longer meant to be an opera—was new. Sounds such as these had never been heard on this earth, and whoever had ears to hear, heard and felt himself quite simply carried away. The conductor Bruno Walter recalled his first *Tristan* as though it had been a religious awakening, after which he "knew that my life had been changed . . . Wagner was my god and I wanted to become his prophet."[323] One of Walter's models, Hans von Bülow, wrote a friend about *Tristan*, he knew "that my heart first petitions the authority of my head for permission to be

---

[322] In German, *"Handlung,"* which might also be translated as "plot." In the 19th c., *"Handlung"* could mean as well any kind of shop or store where merchandise was sold; the verb *"handeln"* means "to trade, to offer for sale," and even "to haggle." The term thus served to engender snide jokes about Wagner's venality.

[323] *Richard Wagner, Die Musikdramen, Mit einem Vorwort von Joachim Kaiser* (Munich, 1978), p. 396.

enthused. Here now, my head has issued its unconditional consent."[324]

Bülow, who administered the work's baptism at King Ludwig's Court Theater in 1865, contributed not only to its idolization, but also involuntarily to its mockery. He was, namely, both Wagner's pet conductor, and the spouse of his pet beloved, Cosima. Her first child with the composer was baptized just two months before *Tristan*. The little girl was named — what else? — Isolde, and bore the surname of Cosima's cuckolded husband.

The secret affair, which soon lost its secret status, left its mark on the reception of *Tristan* insofar as countless prophetic allusions to the triangle in question could be discovered in the "treatment." Wagner was outed as Tristan, Cosima as Isolde, and the hapless conductor as King Mark. Wagner not only set horns on his head, but, as Bülow joked about himself, "the edifice of his cuckolding [was] most splendidly crowned" when his wife bore her beloved Wagner a son and heir by the name of Siegfried in 1869.[325] Commentators and caricaturists virtually did headstands, because the "human dimension," which still in today's media can determine success or failure, was palpable here, and offered professional Wagner criticism fresh fodder daily.

The Wagner-Bülow trinity was not the only "human dimension" to invite malicious trivializing. The Zürich genesis of the opera's subject-matter that lay a few brief years in the past did not go unnoticed. Here too the personal lives of the principals were the stuff of a joke in the manner of Nestroy: the notorious revolutionary,

---

[324] *Ibid.*, p. 389.
[325] Gregor-Dellin, p. 614.

described on wanted posters, as the perfect Tristan finds in the silk merchant Otto von Wesendonck his equally perfect King Mark, who lavishes him with money and silken fabrics, oblivious to the affair unfolding between his music-loving Queen Isolde (Mathilde von Wesendonck) and the music producing Tristan, which is immediately and vociferously made public by Tristan's wife, the profoundly prosaic Minna. What perfect material for a light comedy . . . and already set to music in Wagner's "treatment in three acts!" The critics were in heaven, and their scathing reviews laden with insinuation could sparkle aesthetically as well as morally.

Minna above all nurtured an instinctive dislike of the work, in which, in her view, the most painful marital secrets were broadcast unvarnished. The two titular figures provoked her particular disgust, since Wagner had imposed no compositional limits whatsoever on his representation of their "most exalted lust." In her direct way, Minna felt that "they are and remain just an overly infatuated and repulsive couple."[326]

It was quite otherwise with King Ludwig II of Bavaria, who found in the stammering professions of love the perfect expressive medium for his own desires, to which he likewise ascribed a metaphysical essence: "Unique one!—holy one," he wrote to his Master immediately following the premiere in 1865. "How blissful!—*Perfect*. So seized by delight!— ... To drown . . . to sink—unconscious—greatest pleasure.—*Divine work!*—Eternally faithful—unto death and beyond!"[327]

---

[326] Barth/Mack/Voss, p. 382.
[327] *König Ludwig II. und Richard Wagner. Briefwechsel,* Mit vielen anderen Urkunden in vier Bänden herausgegeben vom Wittelsbacher Ausgleichs-Fonds und von Winifred Wagner, bearbeitet von Otto Strobel,

The intoxication was mutual. The free-thinking former Court Kapellmeister, though thirty years Ludwig's senior, found the arch-Catholic monarch entrancing, and not just on account of his financial largess. Ludwig was quite simply different—gallant and self-conscious at once, and of a half-dreamy, half-idealistic temperament about which Hans von Bülow (Ludwig's "pianist," by the way) was moved to observe that he was "unique; he even looks very tropical, or exotic."[328] In any case, Wagner, who knew how to take the Bavarian exotic (even if Ludwig would not allow himself to be called "my boy" by him) entered into his theatrical game of infatuation, sparing no effusively amorous formula in his replies.

"For me, the only true reason for living," wrote Wagner adoringly at a time when Bülow's wife had long been sharing his bed, "is the wonderful love from the heart of my royal friend that sprinkles down on me like dew—as though from God's lap—engendering new seeds of life in me."[329] Such is the talk of lovers . . . or comedians. Wagner assured Cosima, who became quite seriously jealous, that his love letters, which he sent Ludwig in profusion, were not to be taken literally. It was simply the fact that with that sort of man of power, he explained, one "had to deal as though with the insane,"[330] that is, with humor and the art of dissembling.

The King's intoxicated infatuation (he collected even Wagner's pencils and pens as souvenirs)[331] brought the Master first to a half-timbered villa on Lake Starnberg,

---

(Karlsruhe, 1936), v. I, p. 105.
[328] Glasenapp, v. IV, p. 35.
[329] *König Ludwig II. und Richard Wagner. Briefwechsel*, v. I, p. 30.
[330] Cosima Wagner, Diaries, October 2, 1878.
[331] Glasenapp, v. III, p. 462.

which Ludwig, blind with love, made available to his idol and Madame Cosima for their use as love-nest. Once, when their friend Wendelin Weissheimer came to visit, Wagner received him on the upper landing arrayed in colorfully shimmering fabrics that prompted Weissheimer's amazement. "I say. You greet me like the pope," he called out in jest. Wagner replied smiling with supreme assurance, "Well, I *am* the Pope now!"[332]

And in truth, with *Tristan und Isolde* he did become the "Pope" of the Wagnerites, of whose mystery cult Cosima, as high priestess, assumed leadership. The Tristan drama quickly rose to theatrical non-plus-ultra, and the most prominent Wagnerite, Nietzsche, found it impossible to hear *Tristan* "without suspiration in a spasmodic spreading of all my soul's wings"[333] . . . whatever he may have meant by that. Its creator, on the contrary, was annoyed if *Tristan* was being celebrated at the expense of his other dramas. Once, when his devoted pianist Joseph Rubinstein (who committed suicide following the death of his idol) had performed parts of *Götterdämmerung*, Wagner sobbed "after all, there are a few pretty spots in this, but my wife and all the people always want only *Tristan, Tristan*." At the piano, he played "Isolde's Transfiguration" — "ever only *Tristan!*"[334]

The King, too, who dreamed of expiring in unison with his adored one, at times wished to hear only "*Tristan, Tristan, Tristan*," and peppered his letters with death-intoxicated quotations from the "treatment." Just as the doomed lovers begin to hate the "day's sun" because

---

[332] Weißheimer, p. 311.
[333] Friedrich Nietzsche, *Werke in drei Bänden*, Karl Schlechta, ed., (Munich, 1954), v. I, p. 116. "*Ohne unter einem krampfartigen Ausspannen aller Seelenflügel zu veratmen.*"
[334] Glasenapp, v. VI, p. 707.

they can rendezvous undisturbed only at night, Ludwig wrote his adored one, "the harsh glare of the peaceful day's sun torments indescribably,"[335] which in this case was to serve as announcement of his abdication, against which Wagner counselled at once, for the money stream would then dry up.

Whereas Ludwig sought, with the aid of quotations from Wagnerian texts, to gloss over the royal life he experienced as "unspeakable" with a transfiguring golden nimbus, Wagner himself employed these "wingéd words" with a predilection for self-irony. When the art historian Henry Thode—future husband of Cosima's daughter Daniela—visited him at his Venetian palazzo, it happened that the guest was seated next to Frau Wagner, while the man of the house (dressed in quilted black satin jacket) was forced to squint into the low-lying sun. That was, as Wagner observed, "not comfortable, to be sure, but Tristan and Isolde had suffered the same before him."[336] Only missing was Tristan's cry of pain, "Oh, this sun ..."

Wagner loved to joke even about the moving finale of *Tristan*, in which Isolde breaks out into those words of longing, "Drowning ... sinking," which inspired the deposed king Ludwig to emulation in Lake Starnberg in 1886. Thus, he called out to the orchestra at the beginning of her so-called "*Liebestod*": "So, gentlemen, now for the final cabaletta!" as though it were a comic opera by Rossini.[337]

That "melancholy of desire," too, which Wagner (as he said) had realized sonically in the prelude, he turned to

---

[335] *König Ludwig II. und Richard Wagner. Briefwechsel*, v.II, p. 34.
[336] Glasenapp, v. VI, p. 705.
[337] *Ibid.*, v. III, p. 345.

a joke in comparing it to feeling "like a fish out of water."[338] On another occasion, the *Tristan*-tristesse came over him in connection with his delight in feathered creatures. At an exhibition of stuffed birds in Lucerne, which his children greatly enjoyed, Wagner's attention was mystically drawn to the glass eyes of a waterfowl. "Richard's attention was also drawn to a duck," Cosima noted earnestly, and added his exclamation at the sight: "God, what a look! *Tristan und Isolde*. The whole melancholy of existence."[339]

A comparable melancholy settled over him regularly on fund-raising tours for Bayreuth when he submitted to the gala receptions of adoring crowds. In connection with the *Meistersinger* production in Cologne in 1873, a woman wished urgently to be introduced to him. At their meeting in the Hotel Disch, the composer learned that she, too, as Director of a Rhine area theater had already staged *Meistersinger*. Its remarkable success had in turn awakened her further interest. "The lady," reported Wagner's friend August Lesimple, "asked him 'whether he might not have another such 'comic' opera as *Die Meistersinger*.' Wagner replied (indeed with 'perplexing earnestness'): 'Oh yes, Madam, a splendid comic opera, 'Christian and How-Could-She.' You must put it on. You can do wonderful, brilliant business with that one.'"[340]

Among the phenomena of Wagner's life hard to fathom is the fact that this creative man, comprehensive master of theatrical tricks as well as all forms of humor, never successfully managed a truly comic piece. Laugh

---

[338] *Ibid.*, v. VI, p. 682.
[339] Cosima Wagner, *Diaries*, February 24, 1870.
[340] "*Christian und Wiesollsie.*" *Richard Wagner*, Erinnerungen von August Lesimple, (Dresden, 1884), p. 15.

whole-heartedly as one might at his virtuosically delivered anecdotes, his sarcastic observations, and his practical jokes, his theatrical pieces on the contrary expressed deep seriousness even when entertainment was on the program. To be sure, copious laughter is to be found throughout his operas and dramas, at times jovial and hearty, then again mocking and scornful, or even malicious and gloating, and finally death-infatuated and death-defying. But his audience has learned to find laughter in Wagner's works only since the advent of the modern "director's theater."

He certainly tried. His numerous attempts range from the strained humor of his *Singspiel* (*The Happy Bear Family*, 1838), to the farce in the manner of Kotzebue (*Comedy in One Act*, 1868), and finally to the travesty in the manner of Nestroy (*A Capitulation*, 1870). Artistically, as he knew best himself, all were below par. He simply could not produce anything — be it ever so trivial — that evoked the hoped for response from the audience. Be it *The Happy Bear Family* in which an arrogant Baron von Abendtau wants to marry off his snout-nosed daughter Aurora, or the *Comedy* in which the snuff-taking prompter Barnabas Kühlewind drives an actor named Napoleon Baldachin to despair with sneezing fits, or the *Capitulation*, playing out in the world of the Paris sewers, in which the novelist Victor Hugo has the National Guard dancing the Cancan until he sobs "in delight and emotion" — the audience was never moved to laughter.

Incidentally, Wagner took this defeat with self-irony too. When he submitted the text of the *Capitulation* to the conductor Hans Richter so he might compose spirited music à la Jacques Offenbach with appropriate Cancan interludes for the burlesque, Richter let him know "that it would be embarrassing for him to put his name to it." Wagner observed, laughing, "how heavily one had to atone for such a whim."[341]

All these whims might have been funny, but were not, and engendered rather the opposite effect of involuntary humor. Jokes Wagner dreamed up at his desk blew up in his face. Other planned comedies, among them *Lessing and Frederick the Great*,[342] as well as "three heroic comedies, *Luther's Wedding*, *Bernhard von Weimar*, and *Frederick the Great*,"[343] were fortunately never written. One of his jests, however, one would like to have seen. He "wished," he told his wife in 1879, "to write a comedy for the *Bayreuther Blätter*, in which everyone would appear by name," among them his disciple Joseph Rubinstein, Nietzsche's successor Hans von Wolzogen, and Cosima's father, Franz Liszt. But though "everything" was to be "innocent, but full of nonsense,"[344] it appears he ran into resistance that prevented the *comédie à cles* about the world of Bayreuth from ever being written.

Wagner succeeded with only one comedy, which numbers among his "seven world wonders," is one of the best world-stages have to offer their audiences . . . and leaves precisely in the matter of the actually funny something to be desired. By way of ingenious humor, facetious profundity, and slapstick situations, *The Mastersingers of Nuremberg* offers virtually anything one could hope for in the genre of opera. And still, although Wagner undoubtedly intended it to do so, the work does not really evoke uproarious laughter. To be

---

[341] Cosima Wagner, *Diaries*, December 16, 1870.
[342] *Ibid.*, October 18, 1877.
[343] *Ibid.*, July 2, 1870.
[344] *Ibid.*, September 8, 1879.

sure, there is much laughter on the stage itself — both individual and *en masse* — but it seems strained, and fails to infect the audience.

Grilled Competition. In 1883, the Vienna *Floh* graphically speared and roasted Wagner's attitude toward Jewish composers such as Jacques Offenbach.

Of course this was immediately noted and gleefully spread about. *Meistersinger*, wrote Wagner's poet friend Laube, offers a "comic subject with such serious, wheezing laboriousness, that everywhere one sees sweat breaking out and — quite without humor."[345] The Viennese critical heavy-weight Eduard Hanslick made the same diagnosis: Wagner's work seemed like "a musical abnormality,"[346] whose protagonist, the versifying shoemaker Hans Sachs, is "supposedly funny," but in many passages "reminds one more of an

---

[345] Otto, p. 420.
[346] Eduard Hanslick, *Die Moderne Oper*, (Berlin, 1892), p. 305.

agitated hyena than a merry shoemaker."[347] Thus Hanslick sums up: "What we notice most sensibly is Wagner's lack of humor."[348]

When this singular work was being conceived at Marienbad in 1845, Hanslick happened to be on a visit to his then idol. The critic had been enthusiastic about *Tannhäuser*—as later Nietzsche about *Meistersinger*—and was paying its creator his respects. And like Nietzsche, he subsequently lapsed, such that the excess of their enthusiasm was exactly mirrored in their excessive hatred, allowing neither to dissolve their connection to Wagner, keeping them instead tied to him in "faithful enmity" long beyond his death.

In the summer of 1845, the omens for Hanslick's visit were auspicious. The overstressed Court Kapellmeister had been able to retire on vacation from the Dresden "air of the theater lights," and "soon [felt] at ease and happy: for the first time my characteristic cheerfulness came into play," which manifested itself in the plan "to write a comic opera." The idea did not come entirely out of the blue. Because of his misfortunes surrounding the more serious subjects of *The Flying Dutchman* and *Tannhäuser*, he had followed the advice of his friends, "who wished to see an opera from me 'of a lighter sort.'"[349]

This opera, inspired by the spa waters and readings in history, seemed to him like a continuation of the "song competition" by another avenue. "As it was for the Athenians, a merry satyr play followed the tragedy," wrote Wagner retrospectively, "suddenly during that

---

[347] *Ibid.*, p. 296.
[348] *Ibid.*, p. 300.
[349] Glasenapp, *Wagner-Encyklopädie*, v. II, p. 11.

pleasure trip the concept of a comic piece occurred to me that as a suggestive satyr-play might truly be coupled to my 'song contest on the Wartburg' this was *The Mastersingers of Nuremberg*, with Hans Sachs in the lead." The dichotomy that would evoke laughter would be that between the ironically superior Sachs on the one hand, and "the mastersinger bourgeoisie" on the other, "to whose thoroughly comical, versifying rule-book pedantry I gave quite personal expression in the figure of the 'marker.'"[350]

If during the process of composition Wagner wrote to his beloved Mathilde that sometimes "for laughing, sometimes for crying [he was unable] to go on working," this was also on account of the "marker," for he added: "I commend to you Herr Sixtus Beckmesser."[351] In this ludicrous old bachelor with musical pretentions, whose critical dismemberment through the application of rigid standards entered common parlance as "to beckmesser,"[352] Wagner was presenting none other than his sometime admirer and subsequent enemy Eduard Hanslick—caricatured and exposed to ridicule.

In the fidgety eccentric, for whom art can be only what he himself is capable of, Wagner insulated himself against all those who sought sneeringly to destroy him in the features pages of the newspaper. In fact, the Viennese professor, who had an outstanding reputation and whose influence extended throughout the empire, had developed a very special position in this world. His radical reversal in matters Wagnerian can in part be

---

[350] *Ibid.*
[351] *Briefe Richard Wagners an Otto Wesendonck 1852-1870. Neue vollständige Ausgabe*, (Leipzig, 1905), p. 295.
[352] *Beckmessern.*

traced back to the composer's essay "Judaism in Music," by which not only those directly targeted — Hanslick fell into that category through his mother — were disgusted, and in part to a personal encounter that Wagner had brought about in order once and for all to hold the mirror up to the critic. Invited to a reading of the *Meistersinger* poem in 1862, Hanslick was forced to endure his public ridicule in the libretto. So there should be not the slightest misunderstanding, Wagner had named the marker "Hans Lick." No wonder the target of this ridicule failed to find "this original, thoroughly amusing, even funny theme"[353] (as Wagner characterized *Die Meistersinger*) not the least bit funny.

For this not altogether innocent lampoon, Hanslick dogged the composer with often ingenious, but always gloating and hateful defamation that rose to intemperate statements such as this: "the simplest song of Mendelssohn speaks more to the heart and soul than ten Wagnerian operas in the style of *Tristan und Isolde*"[354] — which Mendelssohn himself, had he still been living, would have blushed with shame over. Hanslick became Wagner's "shadow," and the bitterness of Wagner's later years surely stemmed from the fact that Hanslick and his allies took aim so unrelentingly and entertainingly at his works.

Wagner thought of his Beckmesser, this odd character, worthy of a parody by Nestroy, as an entirely humorous figure, whose errors and mishaps belong in any comedy, without any malicious intent necessarily intended. During the process of composition, he asked his assistant Hans Richter, also a French hornist: "'Do you think this phrase can be played on the horn at so

---

[353] Wagner, *Sämtliche Briefe*, v. XIII, p. 293.
[354] Tappert, p. 111.

fast a tempo? Is it not too difficult?' It was the spot in the finale of the second act where the horn takes up the theme of Beckmesser's serenade. I looked at the passages and assured him, 'It can certainly be played, but it will sound strange and nasal.' 'Excellent!' exclaimed Wagner, 'that is exactly what I had in mind. It will surely have a comic effect.'"[355]

Beckmesser's Model. After having paid court to his idol Wagner in 1845, in the wake of "Judaism in Music," the music critic Eduard Hanslick became his bitterest foe.

---

[355] Kloss, p. 80.

Before the premiere of *Meistersinger* in 1868, generously promoted by Ludwig II, and meanly panned by critic Hanslick, Wagner had acted out the figure of the marker mimetically. "Every figure had to be put together down to the smallest detail, even fully created by him," wrote his disciple Ludwig Nohl, "graphically, in expression, gesture, individuality, and movement. So, in the figure of the serenading Beckmesser sent finally into a frenzy by Sach's singing and marker's beats he demonstrated how he needed suddenly to jump up before the 'maliciously impertinent shoemaker.' It was a positively tiger-like sudden, powerful movement" that Wagner executed, and, as Nohl added, the singer in the role of the marker had great difficulty "reproducing [Wagner's pantomime] with anything even approaching the same graphic vividness."[356]

In *Meistersinger*, Wagner found yet other opportunities for balletic interludes. In Biebrich, when he demonstrated his conception of the dance of the apprentices, it gave his admirer Weissheimer great pleasure "to see him in his chambers perform the merry roundelay with grotesque leaps, while in the liveliest falsetto intoning the song of the apprentices with the words, "The little flower chaplet of finest silk — will that be granted our Sir Knight?"[357]

Wagner had not the slightest doubt that his *Meistersinger* was a comic masterpiece, just as his antihero Beckmesser, inclined likewise to Satyr leaps, actually had something amusing to it. It was just that

---

[356] Glasenapp, v. IV, p. 239.
[357] Weißheimer, p. 99.

The Laughing Wagner

the humor was based not just on irony or the harmless fun of the comic, but rather on mean-spirited gloating. Wagner had experienced this sort of sadism enough himself to pass it along in equal measure to his enemy. Like Hoffmann's Anselmus, everything goes awry for the marker, while what is clear as day to others, he misconstrues ridiculously. His reward is general derision, such as Wagner, first in the theater and then in the press, experienced often enough after performance of his works. For Beckmesser in the end, nothing remains but the "ringing laughter" of the Nuremberg fairground public.

Many consider *Schadenfreude* a German specialty, Wagner among them. He reported an unusual experience from the time of composition of the *Meistersinger* score, in which the laughers were all on one side. On the rail journey to Leipzig, he was tardy re-boarding the train during a stop at Eisenach, and the train began to move just in that instant "when I wanted to step aboard; instinctively, I ran after the departing train, shouting hastily to the conductor, without of course being able to stop it. The departure of a certain Prince had attracted to the station quite a large crowd, which now broke out into loud laughter. I asked if it gave them great pleasure to see this happen to me. 'Yes, it gives us pleasure,' they replied. This experience taught me the axiom that one can at least give the German public pleasure by one's own misfortunes."[358]

With respect to *Schadenfreude* (a concept exclusive to the German language), one must not ignore Lauermann, the otherwise unknown Nuremberg song aficionado

---

[358] Wagner, *Mein Leben*, p. 713. An untranslatable word-play on *schadenfreude*: " . . . dass man dem deutschen Publikum doch wenigstens durch seinen Schaden zur Freude verhelfen könne."

rescued from obscurity by Wagner's feat of memory — *sans* first name, to be sure, but of known occupation. The "no longer young, short, and stocky man, droll in appearance and endowed with only the humblest folk dialect," was a master joiner. Beckmesser's vocal bungling and the nighttime street riot in the second act of *Meistersinger* will forever be associated with this eccentric's name.

How did this come about? As Musical Director at Magdeburg in 1835, Wagner went on a recruiting trip that took him to the old imperial city. Here, in Lauermann, he encountered a talent of the sort that involuntarily offers others amusement. "For Lauermann imagined himself a splendid singer," wrote Wagner, "and proceeding from this presumption in turn evinced particular interest only in those in whom, by his lights, he perceived vocal talent. Despite the fact that on account of this unusual peculiarity he was made the regular butt of mockery and malicious jokes, he turned up nonetheless every evening among his laughing persecutors." Yet it proved "extremely difficult to persuade the man, so often ridiculed and mockingly insulted, to display his artistry, which finally could be achieved only through artfully contrived traps set to ensnare his vanity."

At the inn to which he was guided by his brother-in-law Wolfram and a couple of other wags, Wagner had never been seen, so he was admirably suited to serve as bait in such a trap. Wagner was immediately introduced to Mastersinger Lauermann as the famous Italian opera buffa star Luigi Lablache, who had gained European-wide fame in Rossini roles. Wagner skillfully convinced the suspicious Lauermann of his identity, which was all the easier as his brother-in-law Wolfram knew how "to make the joiner credulous that I, paid unheard of sums for my performances, sought by the employment of special disguises while patronizing public establishments to avoid public notice."

It was soon made clear that "Lablache," who would not sing himself, was all the more interested in learning a few things from this unrecognized vocal genius Lauermann. The "struggle between incredulity and goaded vanity" aroused in the poor joiner ended in the triumph of vanity. Wagner actually succeeded, as he reported with Hoffmannesque narrative wit, "to bring this odd person, who had long fixed his flashing eyes on me in great excitement, to the point at which his muscles went into the peculiarly spectral motions we perceive in a musical automat, when its machinery is wound up: the lips quivered, the teeth ground, the eye twisted convulsively, and finally there came from his hoarse, fat voice an uncommonly banal 'popular song'"[359]—a word, incidentally, which in *Meistersinger*, Beckmesser employs as well.

As Lauermann after his excruciating performance waited to hear "Lablache's" expert's praise, instead "immoderate laughter broke out among the assembled listeners, which sent the unhappy Master instantly into a towering rage. This rage in turn was answered with consummate cruelty by those who up to now had disingenuously flattered him, which brought the poor man literally to foaming." In short, he suffered the same as Beckmesser on the Nuremberg fairground, except that in his case the general gloating at a certain point gave way to remorse, and the inebriated victim was ferried home in a wheelbarrow.

---

[359] *Gassenhauer*.

But this was not yet quite the end of the Lauermann incident. For "in one of those wonderful narrow passages of the old town," known ever since from stagings of *Meistersinger*, Frau Lauermann stood waiting. The energetic lady, only too familiar with "the mocking of her husband's vocal talents," broke out in the "most terrible recriminations against the worthless rascals" who had encouraged her poor husband in his delusion. "But now the wounded Mastersinger's pride reasserted itself, for as she laboriously led him up the steps, in the roundest terms he rejected his wife's right to judge his vocal art, and ordered her most forcefully to keep still."[360]

Scene 5

"My Nibelung Operettas"

In the eight years between the premiere of *Meistersinger*, which turned out a great triumph, and the first Bayreuth Festival productions, whose enthusiastic reception was overshadowed by their financial misfortunes, Wagner devoted himself to composition of his *Ring of the Nibelung*, for which he had had the barn-like theater on the "green hill" erected. To be presented there was no less than "the world's creation and end!"[361] which coincided with the "poem of my life and all that I am and feel."[362]

---

[360] Wagner, *Mein Leben*, p. 114.
[361] *Franz Liszt—Richard Wagner: Briefwechsel*, Hanjo Kesting, ed., (Frankfurt, 1988), p. 207. " . . . *der Welt Anfang und Untergang!*"— another instance of Wagner's ambiguous usage of "*Untergang.*" Does it mean "sinking," "setting," "end," "extinction," "decline," "downfall," or "destruction?"
[362] *Ibid.*, p. 248.

Although its matter was classic tragedy, which evoked comparison (quite correctly) to the likewise multi-part *Oresteia* of Aeschylus, critics lamented the apparent lack of humor here too, for which they compensated with their own pointed jokes. When the novelist Theodor Fontane read the *Ring* poem, he shook his head over "the complete lack of wit and humor, notwithstanding that this lack is made all the more apparent through Wagner's constant wishful attempts to be witty and humorous."[363]

Eduard Hanslick, immortalized in the figure of Beckmesser, went even further when after diagnosing the absolute humorlessness of *The Ring*, stressed its involuntary comedy. "Reading this poetical monster, seasick, one pitches between anger and laughter," he sighed over *Rheingold*. "It is truly fortunate that at the performance itself virtually no words of the text are comprehensible, for the dangerous manifestations of 'general amusement' would surely not be lacking."[364] In other words, the more one understands about *The Ring*, the more risible it becomes. From which almost necessarily followed Hanslick's damning assessment of the entire enterprise: "Hearing *The Ring of the Nibelung* we reached the absolute conviction that every scene could stand the most liberal cuts without suffering the slightest harm."[365] The less *Ring*, that is, the better.

It is the peculiar nature of humor that—depending on individual whim or inclination—it can be deployed either for or against any object: any frailty can, with an indulgent smile, seem endearing; any strength, through laughter, ridiculous. Just like appetite, humor can be

---

[363] Otto, p. 603.
[364] Hanslick, *Die moderne Oper*, "Rheingold."
[365] Eduard Hanslick, *Musikalische Stationen*, (Berlin, 1885), p. 236.

artificially stimulated; one can also spoil anyone's fun or appetite. Just this seems to be the essential point of jokes: they must be neither predictable nor forced. On the other hand, though, they have no defense against systematic humorlessness and abstinence: laughter cannot be forced from a deadly serious countenance, though such a countenance might very well provoke laughter itself.

As improbable as it sounds, Wagner himself regarded his tragedy, in which a bunch of hearts are broken and blood is spilled in buckets—giant blood and dwarf blood, blood of dragons, and human blood—also in a comic light. Like Aeschylus who had added a satyr play as a coda to his tripartite tragedy to restore the stunned mood of his audience with ribaldry, Wagner placed, ahead of his three serious *Ring* days, a not so serious "introductory evening," which he counted among his comedies, presumably not just in jest. At least, *Rheingold* offers up three lightly clad river nymphs and a highly aroused dwarf, who pursues them very much in the character of a satyr. A few scenes later, a bosomy love goddess takes the stage, and sees herself given over to the advances of two love-starved giants, not to mention a notoriously wayward chief god, who, "having compromised himself morally in every respect, is finally rescued by a free-thinking amoralist,"[366] as Nietzsche, the amoral free-thinker, put it.

Wagner could scarcely have seen it otherwise. According to the conductor Felix Weingartner, at the rehearsals for *Rheingold* the composer called out to his artists, "Lighter, lighter, children! We are putting on a

---

[366] Nietzsche, *KSA*, v. VI, p. 17.

little comedy!"[367] The word "lust" is applicable to the dwarf Alberich who, provoked by the scoffing laughter of the alluringly bared nixes, vows "cunningly" to wrest "love's pleasure" by force. Since we find laughter throughout *The Ring*, and indeed "love's pleasure" plays a major role also in its other parts, Wagner could even refer to his *magnum opus* in fun as "my Nibelung operetta."[368]

In addition to the burlesque scenes from the world of giants and dwarves, *Rheingold* offers as a major figure also the Mephistophelean fire-god Loge, whose sarcasms establish an amusing distance from the scandalous happenings. In his widely read disparaging reviews of Bayreuth, which, like their object, were worth their price, Hanslick vied with Loge for the bitterest satire of what he characterized as "a three-hour long musical single-file march."[369] With respect to *Rheingold*, which begins even before Adam and Eve, it occurred to him that one had to be grateful "that Wagner had not pursued the divine genealogy right down to the cow *Auðhumbla*, which by licking salty blocks of ice summoned up the progenitor of the godly triumvirate *Óðinn, Vili* and *Vé*."[370] Hanslick's pranks contributed to the popularization of Bayreuth by scandal not least through their sophomoric humor.

The reputation of depravity preceding *The Ring* wherever it went attached above all to the Rhinemaidens, whose coquettish swimming and diving

---

[367] Felix Weingartner, *Bayreuth 1876-1896*, (Berlin, 1897), p. 39. "Little comedy" here translates the German diminutive "*Lustspielchen*," in which "*Lust*" carries the double meaning of innocent fun, and "sexual desire," or "lust."
[368] Wagner, *Sämtliche Briefe*, v. XII, p. 138.
[369] Hanslick, *Die Moderne Oper*, p. 310.
[370] Hanslick, *Die Moderne Oper*, "Rheingold."

maneuvers, made possible by rolling contraptions, lent an air of vaudeville to the dramatic stage, which in turn provoked its creator—as ballet master Fricke noted following a "swimming rehearsal"—to "tasteless jokes."[371] When one article went so far as to mock the voluptuous trio of Rhinemaidens as an "aquarium of whores," the husband of one of the performers sued the journalist "for defamation of the character of his wife."[372]

Even two years after the festival, an evangelistic village pastor took the composer to task in the Bayreuth Hofgarten. Invited to join him for a stroll, the "visibly agitated zealot [began] preaching a sermon of penance to the Nibelung poet in carefully chosen words concerning his sinfulness, and challenged him to use his influence to defend the interests of the church."[373] Only then did he come to the heart of his penitential sermon, to the actual stumbling block. He pleaded fervently that Wagner "write nothing more in contravention of morality." To Wagner's astonished question what he had in mind, the preacher replied, "Well, the water-nymphs, for instance."[374]

The piece that follows *Rheingold*, named *Die Walküre* for its protagonist Brünnhilde, also elicited moral censure. Wagner's display of flagrant adultery as the instigation and focus of the plot— incestuous adultery at that--was found objectionable. No less than Wagner's favorite philosopher, the pessimistic Arthur Schopenhauer, after reading the libretto registered his own serious

---

[371] Richard Fricke, *Festspielproben vor hundert Jahren*. Aus den Aufzeichnungen von Wagners "Tausendsappermenter" Richard Fricke, (Bayreuth, 1976), June 1, 1876.
[372] Tappert, p. 54.
[373] Glasenapp, v. VI, p. 126.
[374] Cosima Wagner, *Diaries*, September 16, 1878.

reservations. In a marginal notation he put into the mouth of the spousal accomplice, Sieglinde, the words, "Go and murder my husband,"[375] and sarcastically glossed the passionate finale of the act speeding toward the lawless conception of the hero Siegfried with the words, "The curtain falls quickly: not a moment too soon."[376]

On another occasion, the evangelical church lodged a complaint when a certain "Consistorial Counselor K." inquired if Wagner "did not believe that the public at large would be shocked at the conclusion of the first act of Walküre where incest is promulgated, to which Richard," wrote Cosima, "jokingly replied that the experience in Munich had belied that, for the audience there [had broken out] in enthusiastic applause and cheering at the conclusion of the first act, whereas wherever the morality of the matter is presented, they have been bored."[377] The furious protests unleashed among the guardians of morality by Siegmund's much applauded exclamation of procreation—"Brother's bride and sister are you both"—completely overshadowed the fact that not only the beginning of Walküre, but its conclusion too were colored with incest, for in the final scene Wotan, the lusty chief of the gods, strips his daughter Brünnhilde of her divinity with a passionate kiss—mythologically equivalent to defloration. Even though the old lecher refers to his obliging partner consistently as "child," his action provoked no further protest.

Thanks also to this *"liaison dangereuse," Walküre* became the most frequently performed part of *The Ring*, and

---

[375] Schopenhauer made this notation in English.
[376] Otto, p. 171.
[377] Cosima Wagner, *Diaries,* March 14, 1873.

Wagner referred to it jokingly as his "Valk-mill."[378] Another money-producer proved to be "The Ride of the Valkyries," which the famous Berlin circus Renz adopted as musical accompaniment to its equestrian number, "to which the Master," as Glasenapp noted, "gave his permission willingly and cheerfully."[379]

The technical refinements with which Wagner sought to offer his audiences the greatest possible realism proved just as effective. Along with the Rhinemaidens' invisible swim-vehicles, audiences were amazed by the galloping Valkyries projected onto the sky, and by the pair of rams, yoked to the goddess Fricka's carriage, who burst forth on rollers as once had the boar in *Freischütz*. And undisputed high-point of every *Walküre* production was the so-called fire magic with which Wotan, with his divine spear, draws a wall of blazing flames around his daughter, kissed into profoundest sleep.

Wagner's illusionistic spectacles, requiring banks of floating artificial fog, brought Bayreuth audiences to amazement, which was altogether their creator's intention. He correctly assessed the valuable effects of his mechanical dream factory. Following a triumphant *Rheingold* in Cologne he remarked "that Technician Brandt probably deserves most of the credit for it."[380]

Only Hanslick found grounds here too for biting commentary. "But should it really be the highest ambition of a dramatic composer," he asked, "to create music for a battery of magical machinery?"[381] The

---

[378] Kloss, p. 75
[379] Glasenapp, v. VI, p. 141.
[380] Cosima Wagner, *Diaries*, March 3, 1879
[381] Hanslick, *Musikalische Stationen*, p. 247.

purist critic could not foresee that Wagner had thus become the forerunner of the Hollywood film.

The Valkyrie-Tamer. In the festival summer of 1876, the Leipzig *Puck* showed the "Ride of the Valkyries" as erotic circus number.

Although Hanslick, as partisan of Viennese classicism, made light of tone-painting and stage effects, he nonetheless complained dearly when a piece of "magical machinery" failed to function as expected. "Who would not have enjoyed the moment," he asked, "at which Brünnhilde according to specific instructions of the libretto, 'swings herself tempestuously onto her horse and in a single bound leaps onto the burning funeral pyre?' Instead of this, Brünnhilde leads her ridiculous Rosinante calmly between the stage flats giving no thought either to 'swinging' or to 'leaping.'" Almost more annoying to him seemed the depiction of the Rhine, which plays a central role both at the beginning and at the conclusion of *The Ring*. This fateful river, from which the "Rhinegold" emerges and to which it returns, "wiggled," according to Hanslick, "with its badly painted and visibly appliquéd waves like the Red Sea in a provincial production of Rossini's 'Moses.'"[382]

Along with illusionistic tricks, in whose deployment Bayreuth set new standards, Wagner also set great store by realistic portrayal of battle scenes. There were plenty of violent confrontations with and without bloody outcomes in *The Ring*. Giants fought with giants, heroes with villains, heroes with gods, even Valkyries with gods, and each battle proved the occasion of a demonstration of Wagner's mimetic and acrobatic talents. When the duel between Siegmund and Hunding, spouse of the coercively wed Sieglinde, was being rehearsed during the Festival rehearsals of 1876, Wagner was unable to sit quietly in his chair. As though galvanized, he leapt up from the little director's desk and climbed onto the papier-mâché hill where Siegmund was fighting vainly for his life. Ballet Master Fricke recalled that it was downright alarming to those present to witness "the liveliness with which Wagner now carried out the fight on the mountain top." Terrified, the singer in the role of Siegmund called out to the others, "Good heavens! If he now were to go down, if he fell, it's all over." But the practiced scaler of facades did not fall.

Although on previous nights Wagner had been able to sleep only by taking chloral hydrate, and in addition was disfigured with erysipelas—it "swells like a hippopotamus"[383]—"with his swollen cheeks, which

---

[382] *Ibid.*, p. 251.
[383] Cosima Wagner, *Diaries*, June 16, 1876.

were still bandaged with cotton and a thick cloth, he leapt like a chamois into the valley," which led the astonished Ballet Master to the conclusion that "Wagner is and will always be one of the most extraordinary phenomena."[384]

That opinion was shared by Angelo Neumann, who brought *The Ring* to Berlin in 1881 and then toured with it throughout Europe. At the rehearsals of Siegmund's last battle Wagner proved once more dissatisfied with the gladiatorial zeal of the combatants. "Scarcely had the two opponents exchanged sword strokes," observed Neumann, "when something occurred which momentarily froze us with fear. With the agility of an acrobat, the sixty-eight-year-old swung himself onto the balcony box balustrade, and ran full of impatience along the narrow, airy ramp overhang, skillfully balancing himself, up to the first proscenium box, to swing from there onto the stage. There he seized Siegmund's sword and engaged Hunding high above on the ridge in battle. Then, on the requisite cue, he let himself fall hard onto the edge of the chasm . . . all this with a skillfulness that any twenty-five-year-old might have envied."[385]

That Wagner carried on like a youth was astonishing, to be sure, but matched the roles he was acting out: both his heroes, father Siegmund and son Siegfried make their entrances as well as their exits as young men. In the case of Siegfried, in whom one might see a "portrait of the artist as a young man," his boyishness is part of his character. He is scolded as a "stubborn child" by his foster-father, who is named Mime, and like Wagner's own foster-father, is proficient in the arts of disguise.

---

[384] Fricke, *Festspielproben*, 17./18. June, 1876.
[385] Neumann, p. 153.

Because the youth opposes everything this "schoolmaster" tries to instill in him, there is constant friction between them that engenders comic misunderstandings. Siegfried is as "ill-bred" as the little Richard had been, and he relishes being so, with one exception: he accepts every lesson of nature, above all from the world of animals.

Dragon Slayer of Bayreuth. After Wagner has tied up his lampooner Paul Lindau and slain the dragon of criticism—as pictured in an 1879 *Leipziger Schalk*—he can finally direct himself to the treasure of royalties, and attend to the song of his dear little treasure, Judith Gautier, who sits on a branch of the tree as the Wood-bird. Visible in the background is the Villa Wahnfried, from whose windows Franz Liszt and his daughter Cosima look out, while on the door hangs a sign warning: "No Jews Allowed!"

Wagner had found a similar figure, at once "natural" and "amoral," in Grimm's fairytale "about one who set out to learn fear." Although here too murder and mayhem figure, it is really, as Wagner stresses, about "a more cheerful subject." With humor and perseverance the hero withdraws from the fear-inducing educational measures of society. He does not achieve his goal to learn to fear because he is simply too dumb to be frightened by anyone. For this his reward is the king's daughter.

From the quick-witted, ingenuous brush of the Brothers Grimm, Wagner adapted the likewise rather clueless and thus entirely fearless hero Siegfried, "who wins the hoard and wakes Brünnhilde!"[386] With his dramatic poem, Wagner wanted to acquaint the audience with the myth as though "in a game, like a fairytale to a child."[387] But among Siegfried's forerunners we find also that other jokester, who like the fellow in Grimms' fairytale feared nothing and, as the clever variation on that theme, laughingly punishes human stupidity. While the *Nibelung* hero attacks with violence, the other conquers people with their own reflected image. In fact, for the Brothers Grimm, Till Eulenspiegel belonged together with the dragon-slayer Siegfried, whom they described as a "nobler giant Eulenspiegel." Wagner too, a devoted reader of Grimms' *Fairytales*, found in the sharp-eyed prankster a model of his young Siegfried, which "first brought him to the idea of a genuinely German comic opera."[388]

His critics, too, noted that *Siegfried* is comic, though in a sense other than Wagner intended. After the first

---

[386] Wagner, *Sämtliche Briefe*, v. IV, p. 43.
[387] *Ibid.*, p. 44.
[388] Wagner, *Mein Leben*, p. 153.

Festival production in 1876, Hanslick wrote that Siegfried's "battle with the singing dragon borders on the comic,"[389] and his Viennese critical colleague Ludwig Speidel satirized the entire opera as "a puppet show for teen-agers and children,"[390] a characterization inflated ten years later by the Berlin *Nationalzeitung* to "monstrous puppet comedy."[391] The jokers could not guess that Wagner saw things in a similar light. Following a conversation with Wagner, Cosima noted that "Siegfried and Fafner we call Kasperl and the crocodile that wants to gobble him up."[392]

Just as happens in the puppet theater, the heart of the terrible talking dragon is run through violently and graphically, and soon thereafter the evil dwarf also lies in a puddle of his blood because he, who only "mimed" his love of Siegfried, in truth planned to "cut off his head." That the gold greedy foster father was a "caricature,"[393] as Hanslick complained, corresponded entirely to the intention of his creator. Like Beckmesser, his counterpart in *Meistersinger*, Mime represents a type characterized by hyperbole. "He is of small, compact stature," wrote Wagner, "somewhat deformed and limping; his head is disproportionately large; his face is of a dark ashen color and wrinkled; his eyes, small and piercing, red-rimmed; his grey beard, long and shaggy; his head is bald and covered with a red cap." In a word: "weird,"[394] and as though made to order for a Punch-and-Judy show.

---

[389] Hanslick, *Musikalische Stationen*, p. 221.
[390] Tappert, p. 90.
[391] *Ibid.*
[392] Cosima Wagner, *Diaries*, October 15, 1870.
[393] Hanslick, *Musikalische Stationen*, p. 221.
[394] Richard Wagner, *Skizzen und Entwürfe zur Ring-Dichtung*, Otto Strobel, ed., (Munich, 1930), p. 99.

It was no coincidence that the little man with the large head was among Wagner's favorite characters. "Wagner truly excelled in this role," his friend Weissheimer recalled. "He bent over, twisted himself, and produced such an outrageous falsetto it could penetrate stone and bone. In addition he knew how to put on a face that made one think one was clearly seeing the ugly dwarf with his running eyes before one."[395] The *Heldentenor* Adolf Wallnöfer (at the time a member of Angelo Neumann's "Peripatetic Wagner Theater") was similarly impressed by the composer's histrionic abilities: "If he was Mime, he shrank together, slunk across the floor, sang in a croaking voice, and cast a malevolent glance." On the other hand, if was playing the god Wotan, "then his small figure stretched itself, and truly seemed to grow before our eyes."[396] Ballet Master Fricke reported that Wagner had complained for quite a while about his painful buttocks, after having let himself be carried away and indulging in too strenuous a demonstration at a rehearsal for Mime. "In the scene in which Siegfried splits the anvil with the newly forged sword Notung," Wagner had wished to show the singer in the role of the dwarf "how terrified he needed to be by it," and had "thrown himself backward so quickly and with such force that he is still feeling it today."[397]

Dwarf Mime's terror results from his discovery that his adoptive son Siegfried has an astonishing talent for forging, to which he himself, though a trained smith, cannot — through his bungling — compare. "Bungler" is also Siegfried's favorite deprecation for his hated foster-father.

---

[395] Weißheimer, p. 119.
[396] Rützow, p. 162.
[397] Fricke, *Festspielproben*, May 31, 1876.

It was Wagner's bad luck that during the composition of Siegfried in Zürich, a colleague of Mime's resided in the house opposite, and assaulted the musician's ears "all day long with widely resounding hammering." At some point Wagner's annoyance reached a pitch that could be relieved only by a burst of spontaneous creativity. "It was precisely my rage at the tin smith," he recounted later, that "in an agitated moment [inspired] the motif for Siegfried's angry outburst against the 'bungling smith' Mime; at once I played the childishly scolding bluster motif in G minor for my sister, and sang the accompanying words furiously."[398] The ear torment soon came to an end. As Mathilde von Wesendonck reported, Wagner struck an agreement with the noise-maker "whereby he was not allowed to hammer in the mornings — Wagner's work hours."[399]

But traits of his creator apparently went not only into the fearless hero Siegfried, but also into the fearful bungler Mime himself. In 1859, Wagner wrote agonizingly to his father-in-law-to-be, the both admired and envied Franz Liszt, "I cannot adequately convey to you how miserable I feel myself to be as a musician. Deep down, I consider myself an absolute bungler. You should sometime see me just sitting there as I think to myself, 'this just has to work' — and then get myself to the piano and throw together a few bits of wretched trash, only then to abandon it stupidly. How I then feel . . . ! What a deep conviction of my actual musical poverty!"[400] As evidence of this assertion, however, he neglects to reference the work he was composing at the time: it was the third act of *Tristan und Isolde*.

---

[398] Wagner, *Mein Leben*, p. 550.
[399] Barth/Mack/Voss, p. 361.
[400] Wagner, *Sämtliche Briefe*, v. XI, p. 69.

The Laughing Wagner

The extreme mood swings that overcame Wagner during his creative periods also characterized his relation to his finished works. Each of them was equally close to his heart; each character expressed a facet of his own personality, so that he could act them out for his performers, so to speak, from nature. But he might just as easily create a distance between himself and his works that expressed itself in self-irony and sarcasm. Then the jokes that occurred to him about his own creations did not differ substantially from those one might read about him in the feuilletons of the newspapers.

It was precisely *The Ring* that offered him, as well as the critics, ample opportunity to test his wit, indeed on subjects that were for his admirers beyond criticism, let alone satire. In a Till Eulenspiegel frame of mind, he called the tragic colloquy between the god Wotan and the hero Siegfried his "buffo duet."[401] The dialogue in *Götterdämmerung* between their counterparts, Alberich and Hagen, seemed to him as though "two exotic animals were speaking to each other — one understands nothing, but all of it is interesting."[402] He dubbed his music to this scene "concerto for toad, crow, and raven,"[403] and the apocalyptic finale of *The Ring of the Nibelung* (as though a Nestroy comedy) as his "end-of-the-world music hall song."[404]

One of the saddest scenes in *Götterdämmerung*, the parting of the unsuspectingly jubilant Siegfried and Brünnhilde — "Oh holy gods, sublime race! Feast your eyes on this consecrated pair!" — evoked a comical

---

[401] Cosima Wagner, *Diaries*, July 12, 1869.
[402] *Ibid.*, December 27, 1873.
[403] *Ibid.*, July 4, 1871.
[404] *Ibid.*, July 20, 1872. "*Weltuntergangscouplet.*"

association for him. "If you only knew," he said to Cosima, "what came into my head then! In Magdeburg, at the conclusion of a merry overture by Auber, my poodle, who had been waiting for me outside, entered the orchestra, ran up to the bassoon player, kept very still, but suddenly let out a loud, mournful howl. Everyone laughed. I was terribly moved, and ever after I hear that plaintive singing accompanied by the merry orchestra."[405] The musically endowed animal was of course "Rüpel," who, as noted, on account of "several excessively critical statements," was banned from the Magdeburg orchestra.[406]

Wagner shared the strong emotions his works evoked in his audience only partly, sometimes not at all, and with a solid rationale. When the young Felix Mottl worked at the first Bayreuth Festival as an assistant, he heard for the first time Brünnhilde's so-called "Announcement of Death," which evokes tears reflexively from the eyes of every Wagnerite, and so it happened with Mottl, who later made a career as a Wagner conductor. During this fateful scene between the Valkyrie and Siegmund "I forgot all about my work and stood transported," he wrote. "The impression of this solemn scene overwhelmed me so that my eyes filled with bright tears. Wagner, who had observed me, approached and said, quietly: 'What sort of sentimentality is this? We leave the emotions to those out there.'"[407]

---

[405] *Ibid.*, February 5, 1870.
[406] Glasenapp, v. I, p. 234.
[407] Rützow, p. 120. "Emotion" translates the German "*Rührung*," the word on which his childhood nickname "*Amtmann Rührei*," or "Bailiff Scrambled Eggs" was based. Apparently forgotten were those early days when his own sentimentality had been mocked with this sobriquet.

The Laughing Wagner

Wagner generally valued keeping a cool head in the artistic representation of the passions and feelings. He liked to portray himself to admirers as an artisan most of whose ideas ended in the wastebasket, assuming they hadn't already been erased. When a portrait painter by the name of Wittig arrived from Rome to do Wagner's portrait for a medal, the composer said jokingly to him, "do me in the act of creation, with the erasing knife in my hand."[408]

Many a Wagnerite must have been sobered when their pilgrimage route, following a reverent visit to Haus Wahnfried, led to Wagner's favorite, smoky tavern, the "Angermann." There sat the Master at the coachman's table beside the door, carelessly dressed to boot, as Cosima often bemoaned. "He wore the satin suits only at home," confirmed one who ought to have known, the tailor Konrad Weihermüller: "On the go, he was actually quite peculiarly, not at all smartly dressed."[409] In the "Angermann," he chatted with the regular customers, drank liberal quantities of *Weihenstephaner* wheat-beer, indulged himself throughout from his snuff-box, and shared veal sausage and black bread with his shaggy Newfoundland Russ.[410] He even exalted the waitress, described as "tall and slender," to heroine with the sobriquet "Brünnhilde." Occasionally, with a wink, he would flatter her with the suggestion that she "should apply to the theater 'comité' for the ballet."[411] It fit the picture that the mugs were rolled out from the cellar by a "dwarf-like creature,"

---

[408] Glasenapp, v. VI, p. 528.
[409] Otto, p. 470.
[410] Rützow, p. 96.
[411] Cosima Wagner, *Diaries*, February 17, 1879. "R. geht ein wenig aus, unter anderem auch zu Angermann, wo er ein schallendes Gelächter dadurch hervorbringt, daß er dem Schenkmädchen, welches fortgeht, sagt: Sie möge sich doch beim Theater-Comité für das Ballett melden."

Angermann's brother, in whom with a bit of imagination one might recognize Mime.[412]

Wagner himself was not always recognizable, since he liked to enshroud himself in the dense smoke of his cigars, which he was accustomed to smoke in a "very long holder."[413] For fun, he also hid his face under his broad-brimmed Wotan hat. Like the Holbeinesque satin beret at home, this bold headwear was his trademark in public from the time when the revolutionaries of 1848/49, most prominently Friedrich Hecker of Baden, had brought it into fashion. From then on, the "Calabrese" or the "Hecker hat" constituted a political statement, which was even acknowledged in certain dress prohibitions. Liszt learned this when he once borrowed Wagner's grey felt hat, and was immediately informed of the "constabulary complications" that threatened him. Fortunately, as Glasenapp recounts, Liszt managed "just in time [to] replace it with another, inoffensive head-covering, so as not to taken for a 'red Republican' at the border!"[414]

Though Wagner was aware of its politically provocative nature, Wagner remained true to the symbol. In 1863, when he was to be picked up at the railway station in Baden-Baden by his aristocratic friend Marie Muchanow,[415] he first thought he should decline her

---

[412] Lesimple, p. 33.
[413] Otto, p. 428.
[414] Glasenapp, v. III, p. 22.
[415] Wagner surely knew the satirical poem Heinrich Heine dedicated to her with the title "The White Elephant." "*Es lebt im Norden ein schönes Weib/Von hohem Wuchs und weißem Leib,/Dein Elefant ist herrlich, unleugbar,/Doch ist er nicht mir ihr vergleichbar . . .*" "Up north there lives a lovely lady/Tall of stature, and white of body,/Your elephant is grand, it's undeniable,/For me, to her, though, quite incomparable."

company "since I won't look respectable enough in my 'robber hat.'"[416]

Because the god Wotan in his disguise as "the Wanderer" also wears the subversive felt hat, it became the trademark of died-in-the-wool followers. Those Munich Wagnerites who called themselves "Knights of the Order of the Grail," and held "secret conclaves,"[417] wore the eccentric floppy hat. When one of them, the future composer of *Hansel and Gretel*, Engelbert Humperdinck, showed the Master his "large, black, fuzzy artist's hat," he tried it on at once and waxed thoroughly enthusiastic. Humperdinck "absolutely had to get him an identical hat at once; in the future, he would wear no other; this was the very hat he had always imagined as his ideal."[418] Soon thereafter, Wagner received from the Order of the Grail Knights the requested head-gear, which "looked splendid on him."[419]

Scene 6

In the Mystical Red-Light District

At the rehearsals for the first production of *Parsifal* in 1882, Grail Knight Humperdinck served his Master as production assistant, and as a composer was actually allowed to contribute a few measures of genuine Wagneresque "transformation music" to the great work. Under which category this work should be subsumed is a question that occupied the poet for a

---

[416] Wagner, *Mein Leben*, p. 744.
[417] Otto, p. 579.
[418] Hans-Josef Irmen, *Die Odyssee des Engelbert Humperdinck*, (Kall, 1975), p. 44.
[419] Glasenapp, v. VI, p. 437.

long time. To be sure, it was played out onstage and constituted musical theater. But it could not on principle be thought an opera, and to call the piece a drama fell short, for it comprised mystical relationships that transcended the dramatic events in the direction of ethics, as these in turn rose towards theology, so that Nietzsche's term *"opus metaphysicum"* probably suited *Parsifal* much better.

Absent existing categories, Wagner invented a new one, which he called "Stage Consecrating Festival Play." Because he well knew his good-natured persecutors, who would immediately make fun of everything, "he was already enjoying," as the art historian Hermann Uhde reported, "the ingenious jokes this word would again occasion."[420] The jokes were not long in coming, and once more Hanslick led the satirical parade. "*Parsifal*," he wrote, was not at all anything consecrating, but rather at best a loftier magic opera,"[421] such as one might marvel at in Vienna's folk-theaters, though even that seemed to him perhaps an overestimation. Rather, wrote Hanslick, it appeared that the ageing Wagner "had imagined something along the lines of the *Oberammergau Passion Play*,"[422] which no longer belongs in the realm of art, but in that of the itinerant showman. "For me," the star of Viennese criticism went on, "the white-robed, long-haired fool is no Christ, nor the howling androgyne Kundry a holy Magdalen, nor the Bengal-lighted grail-hocus-pocus a Eucharist."[423]

---

[420] Otto, p. 565.
[421] Eduard Hanslick, *Aus dem Opernleben der Gegenwart*, (Berlin, 1889), p. 303.
[422] *Ibid.*, p. 307.
[423] *Ibid.*, p. 337.

It was exactly this, the Christian Eucharist, that, for the Wagner congregation and the Knights of the Holy Grail, was represented in the stage consecrating festival play: here, Wagner was offering an alternative to Communion as it was celebrated in the churches, and, as he thought himself, an authentic one to boot, which took its authority not from religious tradition, but from the persuasive power of art and the "purely human" presented in it. It was no new operatic hero who stepped onto the stage in the figure of the "pure fool" Parsifal, but the true redeemer, restoring to the extinguished grail (that is, the enfeebled Eucharist) its world-renewing power of light, and moreover a highly modern one: Thomas Edison had just invented the incandescent bulb, and already—thanks to electric current—Wagner's grail chalice was glowing with mystical red light.

Cosima was the first to see the entrepreneurial potential of the sacramental work. In the the "stage consecrating festival play," she was handed something that imbued Bayreuth with the sanctity of the sacred, and raised Wagner's art to the status of sublime cult-object transcending all criticism. With respect also to her personally, the opportunity presented itself for an entirely refurbished identity: as the Nibelung "barn" now became marketed as the Temple of the Grail, the adulterous *femme fatale* transformed herself into the unapproachable guardian of the grail, who devoted the rest of her life to vestal office work by the red glow from the holy chalice.

On the one hand, Wagner enjoyed the quantum leap to the establishment of a sect; on the other hand, he made fun of it. Certainly he too saw in *Parsifal* a quasi-religious work, to which the audience made obeisance on bended knee. Nevertheless, for him such was not the exclusive access to this new form of theatrical work. One might also regard it — though quite unthinkably for Madame Cosima — with humor. One could even make jokes about it, not necessarily of the malicious kind that Hanslick and his cohorts resorted to, but with that very Wagnerian self-irony that must have seemed blasphemous to the self-appointed Knights of the Grail. What filled others with sacramental seriousness or enlightened revulsion, always offered Wagner the occasion for private amusement.

Already when he read the *Parsifal* text for his intimate circle where it regularly evoked spiritual ecstasies, he used to divert the emotional overflow into the comic by venturing seamlessly onto the territory of the "lighter muse." "When he had finished, we all sat silent, so moved that no one could utter a word," the sculptor Kietz recounted after a reading of *Parsifal*. "Wagner stood there, opened the piano, and as though to release us from the spell, played . . . 'The Maiden's Wreath!'" It was the song of the bridesmaids from *Freischütz*, a popular street song, with which he had begun his piano studies as a seven-year-old. Now, as if he were back in the year 1821, he remarked: "You see, Kietz, I can do more than just versify; I can also play 'The Maiden's Wreath.'"[424]

Felix Mottl observed the same abrupt change of mood: "After the reading of the *Parsifal* poem," the Wagnerian conductor recalled, "when there were tears in the eyes of all his listeners," he had "sat down at the piano and playfully performed 'The Maiden's Wreath.' 'You see I can do that too,' he chuckled."[425] Performing his own

---

[424] Glasenapp, v. V, p. 137.
[425] Rützow, p. 120.

score on the piano was appreciably more challenging to him. "He tried to play from *Parsifal*," noted Cosima, "and had forgotten nearly everything: 'As a musician I'm no better than a cut-rate dog,' he laughed."[426]

Wagner was less amused, on the other hand, over the moveable sets with which the illusion of transformation from grail forest to the temple of the grail was to be realized. Though the illusion was correct, it did not fit the accompanying music. Wagner, who had already been agitated over having to write "music for the set designer,"[427] had delivered a kind of musical interlude, the "March of the Grail," which ranks today as one of the most impressive passages of *Parsifal*. Unfortunately, however, the grandiose composition concluded shortly before reaching its sacred goal because the rolling sets took too long to complete their travel. "It turned out," Glasenapp wrote about Wagner's intermezzo music, "that for the purely technical requirements [of the sets], it was a few minutes too short. 'So, I shall now have to start composing by the meter!' Wagner exclaimed."[428]

To the rescue rode the Knight of the Munich Order of the Grail. As loyal musical stand-in, Humperdinck delivered the missing measures, and Wagner was content. This did not prevent him from making fun of Humperdinck's imitative arts, however. Thus he advised him "to compose *Egmont* as an opera, taking Goethe's poetry and Beethoven's music."[429] At the first Wahnfried reception of the *Parsifal* festival in 1882, he joked at Humperdinck's expense, though this time with

---

[426] Cosima Wagner, Diaries, July 26, 1878. "*Ich bin ein Musiker wie ein Hund für einen Groschen.*"
[427] Glasenapp, v. VI, p. 438.
[428] *Ibid.*, p. 424. See also footnote 16, above.
[429] Cosima Wagner, *Diaries*, March 31, 1881.

a good measure of self-irony, too. "Bubbling with wit, satire, and mirth," the master of the house entertained his guests with (among other things) the alleged rumor that "'Richard Wagner is a great composer, to be sure, but they say Humperdinck orchestrates most of it for him . . . yet his talent is tremendous.' Immediately thereupon in a variation on the same joke: 'Rubinstein does the sketch, and Humperdinck the composition.'"[430]

The artists who provided him the set designs, incidentally, had been dispatched to Bayreuth personally by King Ludwig II. Heinrich Döll and Christian Jank were part of the team that painted the sets for his private performances and murals for his winter-garden—everything romantically illusionistic as on the Wagnerian stage. Unlike the Bavarian King, though, Wagner was dissatisfied with them. "What do you think of the moving scenery that tippler Döll has painted," he asked Cosima. "And Jank—he looks like a valet who's mixing poison for his master."[431] "'God,' he complained another time, 'to have to deal with such people over the sets of my *Parsifal!*'"[432]

And then the divas! The lone female protagonist in *Parsifal* is Kundry, who in one person must embody both sinner and penitent—Venus and Elisabeth. As a lustful siren, whose mission is to seduce the innocent hero, she must radiate an erotic aura with which the Bayreuth Kundry, Amalie Materna, was unfortunately not endowed. Seeing a blackbird hopping in the

---

[430] Glasenapp, v. VI, p. 637.
[431] Cosima Wagner, *Diaries*, November 13, 1878.
[432] Glasenapp, v. VI, p. 137.

The Laughing Wagner

Bayreuth grass, Wagner observed, "Just like Materna: birds with a good voice are not particularly pretty."[433]

When Wagner Started to Sweat. To the *Parsifal*-composer's chagrin, the robust Amalie Materna, who sang the role of Kundry, lacked the requisite erotic aura, as the 1882 Viennese *Kikeriki* illustrated graphically.

The alternate Kundry, Marianne Brandt, may have been a bit more seductive in appearance, but in enunciation she left something to be desired. "'I'm terribly hot,' she said to me," joked Wagner. "She may be hot; she is just not to ruin my work for me. What is it that she always sings: 'Der Mutterliebe letzten Ku . . .' Let her leave

---

[433] Cosima Wagner, *Diaries*, June 17, 1879.

her cow out of it. She needs to enunciate correctly. The word is 'Kuss-ss-ss!'"[434]

Madame Brandt took her revenge. Annoyed over the Master's criticisms, and bitter at being only Kundry number two behind the clumsy diva Materna—"she pretends to be quite in love with him; that flatters him"[435]—the envious singer placed no restraints on spreading inside secrets. Time and again she referred to Wagner's drinking habits, which had also been passed along eagerly by court musician Franz Strauss (father of Richard Strauss). If the festival horn player wrote home that Wagner had been "so drunk at a rehearsal that he nearly fell into the orchestra,"[436] Marianne Brandt wrote similarly that he "always drinks to the point of inebriation during a rehearsal," which in hindsight, incidentally, she reconsidered: "He is 69 years old, after all, and since 1876 has truly become an *old* man in everything."[437] As to the particular drink in question, it was—as she also added—French Champagne, albeit as Cosima certifies in her diaries always only in "half-bottles."

Occasionally, even his own music no longer pleased the composer. In the second act scene in which the seductive "infernal rose," boyishly dubbed "*Mamsell Kundry*"[438] by Wagner, is conjured up by the evil magician Klingsor, he exclaimed, "I did not write that! That sounds just terrible!" At least so the Munich journalist Felix Philippi, well disposed towards

---

[434] Rützow, p. 180. The singer apparently habitually failed to pronounce the final "ss" of the word "*Kuss*" ("kiss"), making it sound like "*Kuh*," the German word for "cow."
[435] Stephan Mösch, *Weihe Werkstatt Wirklichkeit*, (Kassel, 2009), p. 406.
[436] Willi Schuh, *Richard Strauss*, (Zürich, 1976), p. 19.
[437] Mösch, p. 405.
[438] Cosima Wagner, *Diaries*, August 6, 1878.

The Laughing Wagner

Wagner, heard it. "And only," he continued, "when Liszt, showing him from the score that it was actually written that way, did he call out good-naturedly to the orchestra, 'Children, don't hold it against me! True, I wrote it that way—it sounds awful all the same!'"[439] At a piano rehearsal, at which Marianne Brandt also took part, Wagner laid particular stress on a particular indicated rhythm. "I think I hit the mark here," he said, full of self-irony. "I composed badly, but my rhythm is good."[440]

Beside the erotic bride from hell Kundry, the "musico-dramatic horseradish,"[441] as Wagner called his Klingsor, also calls up refined means to seduce the innocent boy Parsifal into sin. Among them is the crowd of sweet Lolitas who, only just arrived at the bud-stage, go to work as "flowers," and ensnare the pretty youth with their "little ballet,"[442] in Wagner's phrase. Leaving no doubt as to their true function, the Master also called them his "street girls,"[443] whom he happily collectively smothered with kisses when they had brought off their sirens' song and dance to his satisfaction. At the conclusion of their scene at the Bayreuth performances he even bestowed on the "flowers"—alone among all those in the Festival Theater—applause, hissed down by the audience, which already at that time had come to out-Wagner Wagner. Significant in this regard was the statement of a critic covering the Festival for the especially Wagner-hostile Viennese *Neue Freie Presse*:

---

[439] Philippi, p. 122.
[440] Glasenapp, v. VI, p. 618.
[441] *Ibid.*, p. 72.
[442] Schemann, p. 19.
[443] Cosima Wagner, *Diaries*, March 26, 1878.

"Of all Wagnerians, the Master himself remains the most bearable."[444]

Nor was the Holy Grail knighthood, the chaste antithesis to Klingsor's younger maiden blooms, immune from Wagner's jokes. Upon completing the Grail King's part, he remarked to Cosima, "I've shut Amfortas's mouth,"[445] while on the death of the father, Titurel, he commented with the words: "I won't have the old man come again; he would remind me too much of that old gondolier in Venice who was always interrupting the singing of the others."[446] He announced the orderly exit of the chorus of knights with the words, "I shall soon have my gentlemen slouch away to the Radetzky March,"[447] and when at a rehearsal he grew thirsty, he waited for Klingsor's cue about the "chaste knights" before permitting himself a "chaste bitter"[448] from the liqueur bottle.

On the other hand his jokes, which did not eschew the corny, veiled the reality that, as he well knew, he had attained both the summit and the terminus of his "Seven Wonders of the World." This was his *non plus ultra*, after which there was no returning to the lowlands of the subscription theaters, about which he once had joked that a German found anything "beautiful so long as he can hear it 'by subscription.'"[449] As Parsifal withstands every temptation in order to

---

[444] Susanna Großmann-Vendrey, *Bayreuth in der deutschen Presse*, (Regensburg, 1977), v. II, p. 26.
[445] Cosima Wagner, *Diaries*, January 18, 1878.
[446] Ibid., January 22, 1878.
[447] Ibid., January 25, 1878.
[448] Ibid., July 12, 1882. "*Keuscher Bitter*," an aromatic digestif, "*Kräuterschnaps*."
[449] Hans von Wolzogen, *Erinnerungen an Richard Wagner*, (Leipzig, no year), p. 16.

restore the Holy Grail, Wagner seems to have intended his Bayreuth temple to be perfectly cleansed of all profane operatic entertainment: a place consecrated to artistic and human "regeneration."

That, at least, is how the Wagnerites interpreted it, nor was it difficult for Cosima, daughter of a Catholic clergyman ordained in minor orders, to make of it a quasi-religious cult whose highest mission she carried out up to her death, as it were as Wagnerian Pope. That the Master had died only a year after *Parsifal* was no impediment to her movement. On the contrary. His habitual self-irony had only gotten in the way, and not until his laughter had been stilled at Wahnfried could it finally emerge as the hallowed site of eternal worship.

Act Four

"Harlequin Must Die!"

*"My greatest triumph,
would be to bring you all
to laughter in my dying hour!"*[450]

Scene 1

"Tomorrow, we let the Devil loose!"

Wagnerians have always been incensed when *Parsifal* is ridiculed, even when the Master himself was guilty of the offence. They hissed him down mercilessly when he honored the flower ballet with applause and cries of "Bravo!" during the 1882 Bayreuth performances. In contrast to him, his adherents and Cosima were quickly unanimous that this drama about sin and world redemption demanded a pious congregation, that would approach the *mysterium* with reverence.

Wagner himself took a more nuanced view, especially since the sin that initiates the story consists in no more nor less than the laughter with which Kundry mocked the doomed redeemer. As punishment for her unseemly vocal utterance, she is driven wandering through human history without rest until Parsifal redeems her from this curse. Scarcely has her mocking laughter been atoned when the next laughter appears, this time of a redeeming kind: in the celebrated "Good Friday magic," nature, awakened from its wintry death-

---

[450] Glasenapp, v. VI, p. 340.

like slumber, greets the newly christened sinner in laughter. "You weep," explains Parsifal; "look! the meadow laughs."

"All thoughts . . . in enthusiastic excitement." Wagner's toast at the gala banquet on the eve of the *Parsifal* premiere in 1882, as imagined by the journal *Humoristische Blätter*.

Laughter also preceded the premiere of the "Stage Consecrating Festival Play." On July 25, 1882, admirers, patrons, backers, performers, and staff had gathered for a gala banquet in the Festival Theater restaurant to celebrate the work and its creator. "In the most heightened of moods," wrote Glasenapp, "all looked forward to the next day, while at the same time enjoying today's consecrating moment. All thoughts were turned toward this tomorrow in enthusiastic excitement."[451]

On this evening, however, the excitement of the Wagnerians centered rather on an attractive woman, who, hips swaying and head flowing in luxuriant curls, made her way through the crowd, and smiling confidently steered a course straight for her destination. Conversation ceased, heads turned, the name "Judith Gautier" was whispered; some added that she stood in a relation of particular intimacy to the Master.

Hardly anyone could have known that already on the previous day a mute exchange between Wagner and his Parisian inamorata had taken place which the jealous Cosima alone had remarked. Out for a promenade, he had discovered, not by chance, the lovely woman on the veranda of a nearby house, whereupon he, observed by Cosima, executed "all sorts of gestures of deference and penitence. On further intelligence," Cosima adds drily, "it emerges that the lady in question was Judith Gautier."[452]

On that memorable *Parsifal*-eve, as well, it was she who drew the notice of all. Whereas the guests were in formal dress appropriate to the occasion, disregarding dress-protocol she appeared in a worker's linen blouse, with a red cloth around her neck. Determinedly, she approached the table at which the Master was sitting. When he rose and kissed her hand, she broke out in "boisterous, resounding laughter," and without further ado seated herself next to him, where they were at once deeply absorbed in conversation.

---

[451] *Ibid*, p. 632.
[452] Cosima Wagner, *Diaries*, July 24, 1882.

What a scandal this rival's cheeky display of libertinism must have provoked—in Cosima's eyes especially. If Wagner's severe spouse seemed the incarnation of the Restoration, Judith suggested an effervescent allegory of the Revolution. What Cosima lacked, she possessed to excess: youthful charm, confident sensuality, and an impressive bosom. The gaunt mistress of the house, in turn, whose childhood nickname, the "stork," still suited her, sat opposite her husband looking in her black, high-buttoned satin suit more like a widow than the wife of the still alive and kicking Theater Director. With her ash-blond hair done up into a chaste knot behind, she sized up her competition through a lorgnette. Her father, too, dressed in his usual clerical cassock, cast a hostile glance at the stranger, which did not bother her in the least since her whole attention was riveted on the man beside her, with whom she carried on an animated conversation, punctuated by frequent laughter and extravagant gestures. Not coincidentally she was known as "the hurricane" to friends. The Master—at all events—was quite blown over by her.

The well-proportioned "foreign body" at the Bayreuth gala—as almost no one was aware—had a greater right to sit at the Master's side than any of those present, his wife included. For Judith Gautier, to whom the brothers Goncourt ascribed "the inscrutability and mystery of a sphinx,"[453] had not only been Wagner's muse for the past thirteen years and, on the occasions of their infrequent meetings, his secret lover—she had also been a major source of inspiration for the composition of *Parsifal*.

---

[453] Subsequent citations from Joachim Köhler, *Der Letzte der Titanen*, pp. 773 ff., and Willi Schuh, *Die Briefe Richard Wagners an Judith Gautier*, (Zürich, 1936).

When they first met in 1869 at Wagner's villa at Lake Lucerne, the disconcerted Cosima (at the time still the wife of Hans von Bülow) confided to her diary that Judith was "so ill-bred it made me downright embarrassed." She neglected to mention that Wagner, too, indulged in his "ill-bred pranks," among other things showing off for Judith with acrobatic stunts and tree climbing. Since that first meeting, at which Wagner had been infatuated with her, Judith embodied the attractive and life-affirming alternative to the dour Liszt daughter who tortured herself and others. In contrast to her, Judith could offer everything Wagner found seductive: the cunning of a Schröder-Devrient, the passion of a Jessie Laussot, and the tenderness of a Mathilde Wesendonck.

The "hurricane" showed up again for the 1876 festival, upset Cosima's plans thoroughly, and proved herself once more Wagner's aphrodisiac. While he sent her the confession that "I think of the experience of your embraces as of the most enchanting intoxication, of the greatest pride of my existence," he wrote mockingly about Cosima that she "sacrifices herself to the habits of her father," who fancied himself a social lion and overshadowed Wagner with his pianistic virtuosity. In allusions to her demonstrative Lutheranism, Wagner mocked his wife in contrast to the atheistic Judith, whose mother, to top it off, was Jewish: "Love me, and let us not wait for the Protestant Kingdom of Heaven — it will be awfully boring!"

As had once been the case with Mathilde Wesendonck, it was precisely the absence of his beloved that released the creative streak in Wagner. In parallel with the composition of *Parsifal* was his secret correspondence with Judith, whose letters, unlike Wagner's, are not extant. To escape the notice of his strict wife, he burned some of them himself; Cosima apparently disposed of the rest following his death.

To give wings to his inspiration, Judith had to send him expensive toiletries and fine silk underwear. Like Klingsor in his magic garden, Wagner surrounded himself with the aromas of the harem: "I beg you to send me one or two of those charming atomizers." Skin creams, bath essences, and natural sponges, as well as a skin-colored silk comforter which he named "Judith." Should he be chilled during the work of composition, he wrapped himself in the comforter carrying the aroma of his beloved.

So that his wary spouse might not know of these deliveries, the entire lovers' exchange, as Glasenapp discreetly implied, ran through a middleman. The Master, as his biographer related, "was also in direct contact with the Parisian *parfumeurs*, but not under his own name: he corresponded with them as Mr. Bernard Schnappauf, Ochsengasse, Bayreuth, and received their shipments through his trusted barber."[454] In actuality, Wagner's factotum Schnappauf served as *Postillon d'Amour* for Judith's letters, and as cover address for her fragrant contraband.

That Schnappauf was not only a barber and bearer of secrets follows from a Wagnerian comic verse, in which, to the melody of *"Wach auf, mein Herz, und singe dem Schöpfer aller Dinge,"* he sings the praises of the barber of Bayreuth: "Burst open my heart and sing to the bleeder of all things,"[455] in which he plays on the

---

[454] Glasenapp, v. VI, p. 155.
[455] Cosima Wagner, Diaries, November 15, 1877. "*Schnappauf mein Herz,*" a pun on the barber's name regarded as the imperative of the verb

leeches which the factotum recommended as a universal cure. Thanks to his discretion, Judith's delivery service functioned smoothly. His indispensable function as middleman was not an insignificant part of the reason the "bleeder of all things" accompanied his "lord and master" on his final visit to Sicily. Ultimately, even in Palermo, Wagner chose not to forego Judith's regular missives. Life at Cosima's side was hard enough.

On that memorable evening prior to the *Parsifal* premiere, then, not Cosima but Judith sat at his side and held the attention of the Master, who, to the discomfort of all those present, "chatted with her animatedly and with much sympathy." When after a while it came time for a speech, he rose and did what was expected of him, that is to say, performed a duty that seemed ludicrous to him, in view not only of what awaited the audience the following day at the Festival Theater, as of what had transpired within him during the course of the evening.

Finally, this too, burst forth from him, as astonishing as that *Ring* rehearsal in 1875 at which in lieu of a speech, he had mimed the pose of the "hovering genius." The Austrian chemist Friedrich Eckstein, an eye-witness sitting but a few steps away from him, notated the words with which Wagner prepared the mood of his audience for his mystery play of sin, remorse, and redemption.

"The conclusion of this speech still remains word-for-word clearly in my memory," Eckstein reported. "'Children,' the Master proclaimed emphatically,

---

aufschnappen. "*Schröpfer aller Dinge* . . ." bleeder of all things, a pun on "*Schöpfer aller Dinge* . . ." creator of all things.

'Children, tomorrow it can finally begin! Tomorrow, we let the Devil loose! So, all of you who are part of it, see that the Devil gets into you, and you, who are here as listeners, make sure you welcome him properly!'"[456] Whereupon, according to Glasenapp, he added one sentence more, nicely rounding off the whole: "If you do not all go *mad*," said Wagner, "we will not have achieved our goal!"[457] He spoke and toasted everyone solemnly, thinking perhaps of his statement making the rounds in Bayreuth at the time, which according to Glasenapp's credible testimony actually was worded, "the 'Wagnerians' are so dumb one could batter down walls with them."[458]

The guests, who had actually not come to Bayreuth to "go mad," had barely recovered from Wagner's satanic intermezzo, when he began making motions of breaking up. The laughing French woman waved her servant over, took from him Wagner's grey duster and helped the beloved Master on with it. "She did this so meticulously," observed Eckstein, "that finally, laughing brightly, she lifted him, wrapped in his overcoat, entirely from the floor like a feather ball."[459] And he let it happen, despite the presence of his wife, her famous father, and a hall full of curiously gaping Wagnerians. Obviously, the world of flowers and aromas, the voluptuous body and its provocative laughter pleased him far more than the ascetic heaven of the Abbé Liszt and his daughter of the Grail.

Naturally, no trace of this invocation of the devil nor of Wagner's embraces with Judith are to be found in

---

[456] Otto, p. 610.
[457] Glasenapp, v. VI, p. 632, and Rützow, p. 189.
[458] Glasenapp, v. VI, p. 636.
[459] Otto, p. 610.

Cosima's diaries. Cosima was not mad enough to preserve such matter for posterity. The following morning, she noted tersely: "Richard had a restless night; I hear him say softly in his dream: 'Children, I depart, suffer.'"[460]

Scene 2

Züs Bünzli's Sister

Another person suffered, too. Friedrich Nietzsche had broken with Wagner, officially on account of the pseudo-Christian *Parsifal*, which the Master had sent him with a wittily provocative dedication: "Richard Wagner, Chief Church Counsellor." In truth, the break came because, as Nietzsche reported to a friend, Wagner had accused him of "unnatural dissipations, with implications of pederasty."[461] At some point, the philosopher had tired of being the target of Wagner's sarcasms, and chose no longer to rummage through Basel's specialty shops at Wagner's behest looking for silk underwear in the Master's size.[462]

Besides, he disliked the Bayreuth audience, which certainly bore no resemblance to the hoped-for cultural humanity of the future. He called the Wagnerians a "hair-rising bunch!" and bore down with his characteristically gentle humor: "no freak is absent among them, not even the anti-Semite . . . Ultimately, one ought to have a true Bayreuther stuffed for the

---

[460] Cosima Wagner, *Diaries*, July 26, 1882. "*Kinder, ich scheide, leide.*"
[461] Friedrich Nietzsche, *Sämtliche Briefe. Kritische Studienausgabe in 8 Bänden (KSB)*. Giorgio Colli and Mazzino Montinari, eds., (Munich, 1986), v. VI, p. 364.
[462] Sander, L. Gilman, *Begegnungen mit Nietzsche*, (Bonn, 1981), p. 163.

edification of posterity; better yet, preserve him in spirits for his want of spirit."[463]

From then on, of course, he mistrusted the "Spirit" of Bayreuth and the mythological worldview he had just shortly before preached with fiery zeal. In an astonishingly short time, Nietzsche shook off the Wagner faith, and no longer had faith in anything. If up to that point the world had shown him its face transfigured through art, spiritual/aesthetic values now fell under general suspicion. One by one, he now tore away the beautiful masks that had filled him with enthusiasm. Where the sublime had given wings to his fantasy, from now on he saw only the "human, all-too human."

He had singled out Voltaire as leading representative of the movement of Enlightenment, and had inscribed his collection of aphorisms *Human, All-too Human* with the words: "Dedicated to the Memory of Voltaire on the Occasion of the Anniversary of his Death, May 30, 1778."[464] Presumably, the fact that the Master of Bayreuth considered the Paragon of Enlightenment his antithesis played a role in this dedication. By his struggle against church and king, Voltaire had been among those paving the way for the French Revolution, which the loyal monarchist Wagner found atrocious. In addition, the ingenious Frenchman had not only mocked Christianity, but had also satirized the musical theater with the maxim "what is too inane to be spoken, is set to music and sung."[465] For Cosima, who came from French aristocracy and valued its faith, Voltaire

---

[463] Nietzsche, *KSA*, v. VI, p. 324.
[464] Nietzsche, *KSB*, v. V, p 293.
[465] Wagner, *Sämtliche Schriften und Dichtungen*, v. IV, p. 208. Whether this aphorism is correctly credited to Voltaire is debated.

represented the personification of "the demon of perversity,"[466] which she also—not coincidentally—found embodied in Nietzsche.

He, in turn, placed the highest value on their spiritual kinship, and stressed that Voltaire belonged to the "free spirits," among which he now numbered himself. Wagner, on the other hand, called Voltaire the "false god of all free spirits."[467] Nietzsche could hardly wait to send his new work with the provocative inscription to Bayreuth, where it elicited anxious feelings in Cosima, while Wagner himself thought the author "would later thank him for not reading it."[468] He appears not to have been able to resist the temptation, however, for shortly before the anniversary of Voltaire's birth he had an idea how he might repay the philosopher's disloyalty. "Richard," noted Cosima, "wanted to play the prank of congratulating Professor Nietzsche by telegram on the occasion of Voltaire's birthday. I counsel him against it, however, and recommend silence in this matter as well as in many others."[469]

For Cosima and the Wagner literature, there the matter rested, ignoring the fact that Wagner never so quickly let himself be dissuaded from an idea, especially where a joke was involved. His brother Albert, an opera singer, had once gotten a taste of that. "Albert is a great man," Wagner wrote his friend Liszt, which was intended ironically, for he added that he had secretly

---

[466] Dietrich Mack & Martin Gregor-Dellin, "Foreword," Cosima Wagner, *Die Tagebücher*, v. II, (Munich, 1977), p. 27.
[467] Wagner, *Sämtliche Schriften und Dichtungen*, v. X, p. 87.
[468] Cosima Wagner, *Diaries*, April 25, 1878.
[469] Cosima Wagner, *Diaries*, May 28, 1878.

played a joke on Albert: "Recently, by means of a hoax (having to do with a bet), I played him a nasty trick."[470] Unfortunately, the details of the "hoax" his unsuspecting brother was victim of remain obscure.

So it went also with Wagner's Voltaire-birthday greeting to Nietzsche, for final evidence is lacking — much, though, can be conjectured. Certain it is — because Nietzsche has proudly reported it — that in Basel on the day celebrating the great Frenchman, "an anonymous parcel from Paris" arrived, in which he discovered "the bust of Voltaire," accompanied by "a card on which only the words *'l'âme de Voltaire fait ses compliments à Frédéric Nietzsche.'*"[471] One can only imagine how this highly flattering dedication, "The spirit of Voltaire pays its compliments to Friedrich Nietzsche," may have affected the young professor, who had just been compelled to give up his university career for reasons of ill health. He found the anonymous gift "touching, moving," particularly as he felt a personal connection to the fate of this great Enlightenment figure: "Human beings are most implacable in their hatred of the emancipators of the spirit . . . "[472] he wrote Wagner's friend Malwida von Meysenbug.

The Nietzsche literature is unanimous that the mysterious gift lighted up the life of the solitary sick man like a beam of sunlight. "He was so moved, as though Voltaire himself had given him a nod,"[473] wrote his biographer Werner Ross, and Curt Paul Janz thought he noted an "extraordinary joy" on the part of

---

[470] Wagner, *Sämtliche Briefe*, v. VI, p. 150.
[471] Nietzsche, *KSB*, v. V, p 328.
[472] Nietzsche, *KSB*, v. V, p 331.
[473] Werner Ross, *Der ängstliche Adler*, (Stuttgart, 1980), p. 527.

the object of his research, which the "still anonymous sender" had provided him. "Who the sensitive donor was," the biographer concludes, "was never discovered."[474]

The sensitive donor surely had reasons to keep his name secret, for it was presumably none other than Richard Wagner. The year before, he had found an appropriate bust of Voltaire at the studio of the painter Franz von Lenbach. Cosima had even informed Nietzsche, who in her opinion would not be "indifferent" about it.[475] And between Bayreuth and Paris, there was a lively delivery service, whose agents we know were Herr Schnappauf and Madame Gautier. It would have been an easy thing for either of them to expedite the plaster bust via a slight detour through Paris to Nietzsche's quarters in Basel, accompanied by the ludicrously overblown inscription supposedly from the "soul" of a man who did not believe in the soul. If such was indeed the case, the two had done their work well: Nietzsche felt "quite moved" by the spiritual message, and the prankster who had dreamed up the malicious hoax savored his revenge in secret.

Did Nietzsche suspect the true identity of the sender? He would certainly have believed him capable of such mockery, precisely because of Wagner's semi-public insinuation that his disciple had abandoned himself to "unnatural dissipations."[476] The jokes Wagner had indulged in at Nietzsche's expense appeared to the philosopher in retrospect the antics of a clown in whom bottomless malice manifested itself. That is how

---

[474] Curt Paul Janz, *Nietzsche*, v. I, p. 816.
[475] Borchmeyer/Salaquarda, p. 292.
[476] Nietzsche, *KSB*, v. VI, p 364.

Nietzsche characterized it to his friends, and inserted it encoded in his *magnum opus*, *Thus Spake Zarathustra*.

"Shade of Wagner." In the English comic-strip "Ally Sloper," to his visible surprise, the unloved Master finds himself confronted by a noisy clown.

From Wagner's memoir, whose printing he had supervised in Basel, Nietzsche was familiar with the composer's affection for tight-rope walkers, whom already as a child in Eisleben he sought to emulate. "We lived at the market square," Wagner wrote, "which often provided me curious shows, such as the performances of an acrobatic company, including traverse of a wire stretched from tower to tower over the square, which awakened in me a long-enduring passion for similar feats. I actually succeeded in moving quite skillfully with a balancing bar on ropes I twisted together and stretched across the courtyard. Still to this day the inclination to satisfy my acrobatic urges endure."[477]

Wagner played "the little melody to which the tight-rope walkers in Eisleben performed their arts"[478] on the piano for his children, and related the breath-taking balancing acts of two high-wire artists "who met inadvertently on a wire across the Danube, and resolved the embarrassing situation by a somersault one over the other."[479] In Bayreuth, too, he insisted on attending the arrival of tight-rope walkers, in which he was joined by his disciple Nietzsche, who reportedly once accompanied Cosima and her children into town, where everyone "stood around the old town church watching half in horror, half enthralled as one of the members of the high-wire family Knie performed dare devil leaps."[480]

As late as 1878, Wagner was following the career of a similar troupe, of which one acrobat in particular had impressed him. "He was singularly moved by the news reported by his children barely four weeks later," Glasenapp reported, "that the very same young tight-rope walker in whose bravery and skill they had taken such pleasure, and whom he [Wagner] had honored with his friendly words, had fallen from the wire in Regensburg, and had departed the world of the living."[481]

---

[477] Wagner, *Mein Leben*, p. 14.
[478] Cosima Wagner, *Diaries*, October 18, 1881.
[479] *Ibid.*, July 12, 1878.
[480] Kutzow, p. 130.
[481] Glasenapp, v., VI, p. 116.

Nietzsche seems to have gathered all these memories of his now despised Master in "Zarathustra's Prologue." Just at the beginning, as the titular hero steps onto the marketplace of a city, he sees a crowd of people whose heads are turned upwards in expectation of the precarious performance of a troupe of acrobats. A tight-rope walker has just "exited a small door and walked across the rope strung between two towers, such that it hangs over the market and the people." Suddenly, a murmur goes through the crowd, for "the little door has opened again, and a colorful fellow, resembling a clown, jumps out and walks with quick steps after the first. 'Go on, Lame Foot,' he cries in his terrible voice, 'go on, Lazy Bones, Trafficker, Pale-Face! . . . you're blocking free passage for one who is your better!'—and with every word he comes closer and closer."

Arrived immediately behind the poor tight-rope walker, the clown lets "out an infernal scream, and jumps over him who is blocking his way. But he, seeing his competitor winning, loses his head and his footing on the rope. He throws away his pole, and plunges faster than it, in a confusion of arms and legs, to the ground."[482] With his own hands, Zarathustra buries the poor artist whom the "colorful fellow" has driven out of his path, or one might say has laughed to his death.

It seems reasonable to see a parable of Nietzsche's own experience in this picture: the colorfully clad joker Wagner leap-frogs over his competitor, the anxiety-ridden Nietzsche, who loses his nerve and plunges into the abyss of professional ruin.

---

[482] Nietzsche, *KSA*, v. IV, p. 21.

Needless to say, Wagner's penchant for having fun at others' expense did not always end in existential catastrophe. Nietzsche's fall[483] could very well, in a different mental disposition, have ended in a softer landing. Although his victims often laughed along with him, Cosima put up decided opposition to her spouse's habits, not out of compassion for the butts of his jokes, but for considerations of image. She regarded her husband as an incomparable world genius, beyond all doubt a sublime artist of the first rank, whom it behooved to radiate the cool self-possession of a marble bust. Her father, Franz Liszt, who valued aristocratic formalities, was to serve as model.

But Wagner put up stiff resistance, not least because such cool reserve conflicted with his effervescent temperament. The composer Wilhelm Kienzl, who met the Master in the late 1870's in Wahnfried, bore witness to his "boyish liveliness," as well as a sense of humor that, accompanied by vivid mimicry, "flowed unusually fully." To be sure, those in his company also got a taste of less pleasant examples. "One soon grew used to the fact," according to the composer of the *Evangelimann*, "that sooner or later no one present was immune; a retort would only serve to make one ridiculous, since it could never have the effect of negating his joke. Of course the name or status of the butt of his joke was a matter of complete indifference to him."[484]

Here too, Wagner ran up against Cosima's etiquette: status and name meant everything to her, and even at the outset of their love relationship, she divided up his friends according to social status, so that those who did

---

[483] "Der Fall Nietzsche," an untranslatable pun alluding to Nietzsche's *Der Fall Wagner* (*The Case of Wagner*).
[484] Otto, p. 570.

not measure up were no longer granted access to the Master. It was not only Peter Cornelius, once Wagner's closest friend, who complained about it. Cosima's concept of the household establishment of a genius, over which she was to preside, followed exactly the model of those Parisian salons in which aristocracy, clergy, and cultural personalities gathered to enjoy *haute cuisine* and gossip about *haute société*. What she had experienced as a child in the salon of her mother, Countess Marie d'Agoult, she reconstructed in Wahnfried's halls. She knew only too well that the real focal point, her composer husband Richard, did not at all fit into such affected company, and for that reason did all she could to re-educate him to match the image of her ideal.

Occasionally, she herself assumed the central position, and held court like an uncrowned princess. Her husband remained the draft horse, to be sure, but Cosima held the reins. A dream of Wagner's, registered in her diary barely half a year before his death, expressed the unpleasant feeling of having lost control. "Richard has a restless night," she wrote, "he dreams about Wahnfried, which has been completely changed about; everywhere, arrangements in preparation for guests, and he, asked who he is, loudly and angrily says his name, at the same time hearing me laugh in an adjoining room."[485]

If Cosima had counseled her husband against pursuing his "joke" with Nietzsche, it was not out of a wish to protect the former disciple, whose "perversion"[486] they thought to have seen through, but rather because she had no use for jokes of the Wagnerian stamp.

---

[485] Cosima Wagner, *Diaries*, September 8, 1882.
[486] *Ibid.*, September 9, 1879.

The Laughing Wagner

Accordingly, she did her best to drive that Saxon humor out of her husband and Master. She regarded as simply inappropriate, for instance, that—in the words of an adherent Karl Heckel—to a threefold "Hip, hip, Richard Wagner!" he responded "in a hearty Saxon dialect, 'But Holy Jeeesuuss! I am no prince!'"[487]

"Shut your trap! . . ." At a performance of *Meistersinger* in Vienna in 1870, Wagner gave them a taste of his coarse Saxonisms.

---

[487] Elisabeth Förster-Nietzsche, *Wagner und Nietzsche zur Zeit ihrer Freundschaft*, (Munich, 1915), p. 395. "*Herr Jesses*," is the expletive in Saxon dialect.

In vain, Cosima pursued a life-long campaign against his Saxonisms. Wagner insisted on this idiosyncrasy no doubt also because it was only in his native tongue that his humor really came into its own, which as his friend Friedrich Pecht said was "of a charming inexhaustibility made even more amusing by his Saxon dialect."[488] He was especially fond of doing impressions of Leipzig and Dresden characters like the set designer Heine, which did "not especially" please Cosima. He countered her expressions of displeasure with the admonition, which she recorded: "'You do not like my friend. Well, but, that is the world that brought forth *Tannhäuser* and *Lohengrin*.' When I laughed, he went on, 'And that is exactly how it was with the *Nibelungs* and with *Tristan*, not a hair's breadth of difference.'"[489]

Along with his Saxonisms, Cosima also found his exuberance not merely inappropriate, but downright offensive. Spiritual edification, yes, of course, even light-hearted pronouncements in the manner of Hans Sachs were permissible. But coarse jokes and barbarous indulgences, whether of an alcoholic or other nature, were frowned on. Wagner, the beer and champagne aficionado, who visited the Angermann every day, and could rattle off a Leporello-like catalogue of favorites, had to marshal his whole power of invention to defend his cheerful nature against the mistress of the house. He succeeded so well in this that it escaped the notice even of his biographers.

Cosima, too, was in the dark (or chose doggedly to remain so) about who Wagner was when he was not being "Wagner" — perhaps because things had once been the same for her. Wagner's spouse, who went

---

[488] Kloss, p. 37.
[489] Cosima Wagner, *Diaries*, June 6, 1871.

down in the books as Bayreuth's Keeper of the Grail, had not been born the high lady she seemed to her reverential contemporaries. After her parents separated, they avoided their three children for years lest they be reminded of their former partners. Cosima had lived primarily feeling she had a distant, world-renowned piano virtuoso for a father, and a no less distant aristocratic mother, and as such was actually depicted in the leading role of a social novel by Balzac.

The reputations of both were clouded by the fact that Franz Liszt as well as Marie d'Agoult had embraced irregular love lives, which in the previous century had been dubbed *libertinism*. Still in the time of Bayreuth, her father lived in what was regarded as "concubinage" with an immensely wealthy and bigoted Russian, who kept him on a short leash, which led Wagner to joke "That's how it goes when a female rules over a man."[490]

And concerning the life-style of her mother, Cosima might read in Balzac's novel *Beatrix* how the eponymous heroine, gifted with a quick wit and not entirely flawless beauty did not shrink from any faithlessness so long as it served to satisfy her vanity. Like her real-life model, Beatrix abandoned husband and children to follow a musical genius off into the blue. When this escapade crashed and burned, she led astray into adultery a youth whom, as a formality at the behest of her next lover, she replaced with her husband. In this, Balzac's Beatrix acted as cold-bloodedly as the real Madame d'Agoult, who left the children begotten

---

[490] *Ibid.*, January 10, 1882. "*So geht's, wenn ein Frauensbild ein Mannszimmer beherrscht.*" Wagner's untranslatable joke rests on the interchanging of the deprecatory suffixes of "*Frauenzimmer*" and "*Mannsbild.*"

with Liszt to their fates, to return "ruefully" to the luxurious life of a *femme fatale*.

"She is the perfect example of a wicked, shiftless female character, coquettish out of a pathetic need for recognition," wrote Balzac, "a woman without head or heart, recklessly immoral, who loves always and only herself." Since Cosima had abandoned her husband, Hans von Bülow, and three children for the sake of a famous musician, it seems likely that Balzac's Beatrix, like her real-life original, affected Cosima like a self-fulfilling prophecy.

Parallels between mother and daughter ended the moment the latter wed Richard Wagner, and not necessarily to his advantage. To be sure, she towed his *Dutchman's* ship into a safe harbor, but she chained it so fast that he often felt like a prisoner. Her bad conscience, of whose torments she continually reminded her new life's companion, served her as catalyst to self-realization. For Wagner, on the other hand, the joys of adultery soon faded in the turbulent family idyll with five children, out of which emerged a new Cosima, whom previously he could not have imagined.

The seductress of Parisian sophistication became now a severe mother, conscious of the exclusive status Wagner had achieved through his stage works. It was time to make up for what he himself had neglected, namely converting his prominent status into influence, power, and above all money. Bayreuth would see to that, and Cosima would see to Bayreuth.

And who saw to the love-needy Richard? He soon missed the tenderness with which Bülow's spouse had tearfully drawn him to her, and reluctantly, he grew accustomed to the fact that the discipline of the two governesses who had once drilled Cosima in Paris began to make itself felt first in her and then throughout their joint household. In particular, she watched over his table manners like a hawk—something the Rhinemaiden Lilli Lehmann, a guest at Wahnfried, took note of. "Things were not always made easy" for the Master, she wrote in her memoir, "when one sought to 'educate' him, the 62-yeard-old, if, for example, he did not employ his knife in a sufficiently English manner at a meal, which led to dinners often coming to an unexpectedly abrupt end."[491]

Cosima shone in the role of the veneration-demanding lady, at whose feet lay the aristocracy of Europe. No less, though, did she fancy herself as at once humble and implacable parent who ceaselessly "sacrificed" herself for her own. There was no room any longer for the sort of love Wagner had rhapsodically immortalized in his works. That he sought satisfaction elsewhere was not unknown to Cosima; that this further weakened his position with respect to her, he was only too aware. In a late work, Nietzsche put into the mouth of the lady who behaved like a prudish dominatrix the words, "All heroes will go to their ruin with me."

Wagner bore it all with humor. Curiously enough, it is in Cosima's own diaries that the encrypted jokes and taunts aimed at her have been preserved. She either did not get his allusions, or consciously ignored them to avoid strife. But she did indeed write down how Richard took aim at her religious pretentions, and

---

[491] Lilli Lehmann, *Mein Weg*, (Leipzig, 1920), p. 228.

mocked her absurd enthusiasms for martyrdom and renunciation. Most amusing he found her disposition to knowing everything better; this lent her an air, heightened by her pince-nez, of the secondary school teacher.

Following a meeting with her, Ferdinand Lassalle, one of the founders of the social democratic movement, noted similarly that Cosima had attained "the educational level approximately of a French girl's boarding school," while the novelist Romain Rolland gently mocked that the lady, inclined to "superficial brilliance," concerned herself "particularly with serious matters—on reflection."[492] The gaps in her knowledge were unmistakable and appear clearly in her diaries. Only rarely does the Mistress of Bayreuth recognize the classical quotations with which Wagner lards his monologues; mostly, she even reproduces passages from his own works inaccurately. Nevertheless, he let her have her illusions, and limited himself to ironic barbs like the one concerning the bust of her installed in Wahnfried: "She looks as though she is saying, 'I have something more to say!'"[493]

Cosima also records a telling critique, the more significant for Wagner's having pronounced it openly in the presence of a third person, his *Parsifal* conductor, Hermann Levi. She herself had provided the occasion when she attempted to instruct the cultured guest on the subject of *Parsifal*. This apparently embarrassed her spouse sufficiently that the critical statement with which Cosima several days later "laughingly" reproached him had slipped from his memory —*viz.*,

---

[492] Köhler, p. 594.
[493] Cosima Wagner, *Diaries*, added below the entry for November 28, 1879 as "unspecified date."

"that he likened me in my conversation with Kapellmeister Levi to 'Maid Züs' ..."[494]

Guardian of the Grail. In 1905, *Der Kladderadatsch* pictured Cosima as a grotesque widow.

Maid Züs is known as the major figure in Gottfried Keller's ironic story *The Three Righteous Comb-makers*, which Wagner liked to read aloud to the family circle,

---

[494] *Ibid.*, August 6, 1878.

partly because he knew the author well from his days in Zürich, partly because he thought it instructive for certain of his listeners. Thus, there could have been no doubt about the heroine's nature and doings in the minds of the married couple.

Keller's heroine, Züs Bünzli from Seldwyla offers the perfect example of a self-righteous virgin of limited horizons. The 28-year-old has already sampled the greatest variety of men, without being able to keep a single one, wherefore she now praises abstention to the skies. This does not deter the three comb-makers from burning with love for her, though in the intoxication of their ardor they overlook the fact that the lady, charming from afar, on closer view turns out to be a pedantic know-it-all, who tirelessly tries to instruct those around her in the manner of a schoolmarm.

The irony of the story lies in the fact that Züs Bünzli, who knows all things better, does not possess so much as "the education of a girl's boarding school." She is thus dumb, in so many words, and what is more, highly conceited. But this does not really occur to the three righteous comb-makers who are in competition with each other for her love, since they too suffer from ignorance, except with respect to the objects of their profession.

When the maiden finally wants to instruct them even about their very own métier—the manufacture of combs—and maintains that the unicorn provides people "the snow-white ivory and the turtle, its transparent bones," her admirers, for once, dare to correct her. "'In this you are certainly mistaken,' they explain; 'ivory comes from elephant teeth, and the tortoise-shell combs are made from the shell, not the bones, of the turtle!' Züs turned fire-red and replied curtly: 'But that is still debatable, for you have surely not seen where these things come from; you just work the pieces. I am usually rarely mistaken ...'"

In his comparison, Wagner may well have had in mind that last sentence with which Gottfried Keller sums up as it were the essence of the misery that ignorant know-it-alls call down upon their fellow humans. The combmaker, namely, who "won the race" — a race was indeed run for her hand — got "not much joy out of it; for Züs gave him no glory, but domineered and oppressed him, and regarded herself as the singular fount of all things good."

Strolling through Wahnfried's ballroom, Cosima chided her husband for having drawn the comparison. He quickly sought to justify himself. In a few words, he explained the meaning he attached to the joke about his wife. "Oh!" he replied, "it is my salvation, this gift of turning the most serious matters spontaneously into nonsense. That's how I have managed to keep myself from the abyss."

Scene 3

The Praying Mantis

Their differing attitudes towards what constituted "marital love" was one of the many "abysses" Wagner was confident he could bridge over. While Wagner's conception of marriage can easily be reconstructed, Cosima's turns out to be more complicated: on the one hand, she saw herself as loving wife, thus countenancing no other goddesses alongside her; on the other, she cultivated an image of herself approaching perilously that of a saint.

Already as a child Cosima had pursued a mystical cult in which virginity and Christ's blood played their parts, and later felt—having betrayed Bülow with the irresistible theater genius—an inner calling to the role of the great penitent, Mary Magdalen. In her diaries there are countless references to those religio-masochistic self-accusations, peaking in the confession that "the more deeply I suffer, the more powerfully this strange lust for suffering manifests itself within me"[495]—for that matter making others suffer, too, for she asks herself in all seriousness if it "might perhaps be better and more beneficial for me and others if I were a bit cruel."[496]

One can well imagine the discomfiture of the sensualist Wagner over Cosima's "lust for suffering" coupled with a little cruelty. He was no stranger to self-torment, to be sure, but not in the matter of sensuality, especially not as a substitute for it. As it dawned on him that this was precisely Cosima's intention, he exalted the sensual Judith as his aphrodisiacal idol, and resorted at home to gallows humor. All the while Cosima, the holy aspirant, oblivious, diligently recorded his witticisms about her ecstatic asceticism.

Cosima long held her husband's comparison of her to the soul-destroying Züs Bünzli against him. When she reminded him of it three years later, he brought into the discussion one of her female icons: "As I compare myself to Maid Züs, he says: 'Today, it is really more

---

[495] *Ibid.*, February 27, 1876.
[496] *Ibid.*, February 23, 1869

Catherine of Sienna!"[497] whereby he alluded to his wife's latest role model. On a visit to Siena the previous year, in a basilica she had found a fresco in which she saw reflected her own mystical disposition. It showed the saint, pale and emaciated, with abstracted gaze and clearly visible stigmata, wherein Cosima perceived a "total, realized inspiration." She added rhapsodically, "I find it difficult to look at anything else after this."[498]

While Cosima continually enthused over her new patron saint, who advocated virginity and could display her bleeding stigmata, Wagner kidded her about this superstitious aberration. One morning, when she was marked with countless mosquito bites, he joked that she too had now gotten her stigmata.[499] In order not to have forgo the "moving" sight of her favorite saint in Palermo, the destination of their trip to Italy, Cosima, without Wagner's knowledge, had acquired a miniature saint's image, which very soon fell into his hands. "The portrait of Saint Catherine he found among my things," she noted in a fit of pique, "evoked from him the exclamation, 'Saints above!, to have such females around one!'"[500] Exactly whom he meant by this goes unrecorded.

At last, he let the cat out of the bag: having teased Cosima about Catherine of Siena even at cards,[501] he permitted himself the observation that she was already beginning to resemble the ascetic mystic: "Jokingly, Richard calls me Saint Catherine."[502] Wagner's attitude

---

[497] *Ibid.*, August 10, 1881.
[498] *Ibid.*, August 30, 1880.
[499] *Ibid.*, September 1, 1880.
[500] *Ibid.*, September 13, 1880.
[501] *Ibid.*, September 20, 1880.
[502] *Ibid.*, January 21, 1882.

toward the saint finally grew darker when he learned that the pious lady had been excessively engaged in church politics. Wagner angrily interrupted a reading about her. "The subject" was, namely, as Cosima wrote, "not a pleasant one" for him; "he was not interested in the association of the saint with political concerns." Only then did he say openly what presumably had been on his mind since Siena: "The best one can say is that a woman like that is dumb."[503]

For the most part, Wagner took advantage of his jokes, called Cosima the *"mater colorosa"*[504] as she sat for a portrait with a painter, and reacted furiously when she repeated her litany "how I made every effort never to be at odds with him in anything, whereupon he leapt vigorously out of bed saying: I thought I was virtue itself."[505] But she thought so herself—she, who apparently like Kundry wished just to "serve, serve," and in truth held the whole Bayreuth enterprise, including its living trade-mark by the bit. At the same time, she insisted that all in Wahnfried proceed piously and genteelly, as in a model household, with all the cumbersome consequences this entailed for Wagner.

Since he was unable to deal with the problem seriously, he resorted to gallows humor and joked about her "Catholic face, whereby he always teasingly put on an ecstatic expression, which apparently he notices in me from time to time,"[506] or made snide remarks about her "aspirations to sanctity,"[507] and her accompanying

---

[503] *Ibid.*, January 4, 1882.
[504] Glasenapp, v. VI, p. 310. A pun alluding to the *"mater dolorosa"* from the *"Stabat Mater"* text. *"Colorosa"* presumably because Cosima was being painted.
[505] Cosima Wagner, *Diaries*, November 30, 1882.
[506] *Ibid.*, October 15, 1878.
[507] *Ibid.*, January 30, 1882.

pedagogical goal: "You are surely raising the children to be saints; you give the eldest the pension, and the others have to run about with pale blissful faces!"[508] There were also attempts at conversion, to initiate her husband into her faith. "When I speak to Richard about [Thomas à Kempis's] *The Imitation of Christ*, and say I want to know whether he would like it, he replies, 'I am stuck in the devil of art!'"[509]

In the course of their joint reading of Goethe's *Wilhelm Meister*, Cosima, "greatly moved," came across the resolution of the young Hilarie to renounce carnal love entirely, which led her husband to reply, "Yes, yes, I know, you would very much like to institute that kind of regime of renunciation here, I know, however . . ." If pressed, one could imagine how Wagner's sentence might have gone on. Prudently, he bit his tongue, on which Cosima made the bitter-sweet comment, "He interrupted the joke. Certainly, I am committed above all to sweeping away every vestige of desire, and to do penance in this way until I will have been able to atone."[510]

Since Cosima, true to Christian teaching, regarded carnal lust as the root of the sin she and Wagner had committed in common, "desire" became for her a perennial stumbling block. As a result, the thirty-year-old appears to have reduced sexual relations to the unavoidable; her guilt complex spoiled every pleasure unconnected with self-flagellation. "For me," she confessed to her diary, "every form of desire has disappeared. For Richard, it still rules,"[511] which filled

---

[508] *Ibid.*, March 21, 1870.
[509] *Ibid.*, January 14, 1881.
[510] *Ibid.*, August 6, 1869.
[511] *Ibid.*, November 11, 1870.

her with deep anxiety. "Passionate desire on Richard's part instills a mood of melancholy in me; I would most like to change and . . . take in only radiant glances; I have suffered too much to be able to experience other pleasures!"[512]

It seems, though, that Wagner constantly asked himself why just he should have to suffer on account of her abstinence complex. No thinker before him had made carnal love so central to his world-view; no musician had dared render the ecstasies of sexuality more palpably in music. And of all people, his own wife in her prime confided to him, "I think I am now ripe for the convent,"[513] and wrung from him on another occasion the sarcastic lament, "Shall we found a convent?"[514] Until then, he proposed, she should don a "hair shirt." He eschewed the necessary *"austérités"* (penances) himself; he would rather [have] oysters" (*Austern*)[515] on the table, he punned. And, when he did again embrace his austere wife, with desperate humor he asked, "Do you actually still have a body?"[516]

The enforced renunciation weighed more heavily on him than Cosima might have imagined. Alluding to *Wilhelm Meister*, in which sexual abstinence forms the central theme, he warned her seriously "just not too much [emulation of] Makarie," the pious apostle of chastity; "I ever fear from you a holy disaster."[517] The fear of suffering a "holy disaster" through Cosima's asceticism and zealous piety seems to have pursued

---

[512] *Ibid.*, February 14, 1871.
[513] *Ibid.*, November 12, 1870.
[514] *Ibid.*, August 4, 1878.
[515] *Ibid.*, July 31, 1878.
[516] *Ibid.*, April 14, 1878.
[517] *Ibid.*, April 13, 1870. Untranslatable pun: *"ein heiliges Unheil."*

Wagner even into his unconscious. Instructive is that dream he recounted to Cosima three months before his death in Venice: "He was wearing a remarkably large hat, from which tassels hung down very annoyingly; he tried to rearrange them, when a giant locust fixed him with its gaze, thoroughly terrifying him."[518]

The meaning of this curious image is perhaps illuminated by the knowledge that Franz Liszt had taken minor orders. Plausibly, in Wagner's dream-life, Liszt's title of Abbé was associated with the priest's heraldic emblem depicting the clerical hat with two tassels. In any case, his father-in-law had announced a visit, which had always evoked apprehension in Wagner, knowing how much Cosima loved to measure him against her father. Since Wagner resisted her attempts to educate him — in the dream, he tries to rid himself of the annoying, vision-obstructing tassels — Cosima threw him a stern look, which in the dream appeared as the long, scrawny body, composed only of skin and chitin, of a giant locust, which resembles a praying mantis. That the female *mantis religiosa* additionally delights in devouring her little man after copulation was surely known to the dreamer.

In fact, hundreds of his dreams are recorded in Cosima's diaries, in which his true mental state, unfiltered through the censoring lens of the diarist, can be read. Many of them follow so transparent a logic one is tempted to attribute them less to his unconscious than to a willful effort to fill his wife in on unutterable truths by way of apparently absurd fables.

Among these was the perennial frustration that she preferred her role as unapproachable high priestess of

---

[518] *Ibid.*, November 15, 1882.

his cult to that of (in Goethe's words) her husband's *"Bettschatz."*[519] What Wagner could not raise openly without provoking marital storm,[520] of which there was quite enough, he told her as an innocuous dream story. If its message was scarcely understandable to a reader of the diaries, it was for its addressee as well.

In 1878, the sixty-five-year-old Wagner recounted a dream to her in which Cosima and her father ran away from him "so fast he could not catch up with [her]." When she had returned in the evening (still in the dream), Wagner noted a bizarre transformation in the marital bedchamber: "Richard melancholy; in the beds lots of watering cans and sheet-metal implements!"[521]

The explanation — as Cosima might have surmised — is supplied by an episode from the preparations for the first Bayreuth performances. As is well known, in *Rheingold*, the treasure hoard of the Nibelungs figures centrally. The question how to represent a considerable quantity of golden jewelry, utensils, and weapons without breaking the bank was resolved by Wagner in an elegant way, as Ballet Master Fricke noted down. "Wagner assigned me the task of driving to town with Lady Cosima to rent from a copper-smith or plumber the requisite [items] for the *Nibelungen* hoard for today's rehearsal. At Vogel the plumber's we found the hoard in the form of 44 objects: oil cans, tin boxes, sieves, cake forms, buckets, watering cans, pots, and so on."

Thus, Wagner's dream message to Cosima might very well have been: the treasure that lies beside me in bed

---

[519] "Bed-treasure."
[520] Cf. *Walküre*, Act II, Scene 1, *"Der alte Sturm, die alte Müh'!"*
[521] Cosima Wagner, *Diaries*, November 12, 1878.

is as fake as the metal stuff we put forth as real treasure in *The Ring of the Nibelung*.

Scene 4

"From Heaven through World to Hell"

Wagner's death on February 13, 1883 came as a surprise to everyone, only not to himself. Again and again he had suggested this possibility, even wished for it. His drawn-out demise might be named, after a famous novel, "Chronical of a Death Foretold."

At any rate, with it, he spared himself the Europe-wide celebrations of his seventieth birthday that awaited him on May 22, 1883. The anniversary would have brought him the greatest triumph of his life, for with the successful performance of *Parsifal*, which garnered a profit of 150,000 Marks, his improbable Bayreuth project had finally been solidified. For the torch-light parades, the panegyric serenades, the laurel wreaths, and the doctoral hats the Master himself would most likely have had only snide remarks left to dole out.

Already in 1881, the year before the *Parsifal* premiere, he had confessed his general weariness with life. "I have departed the German Empire," he told her, disillusioned over the withholding of official subsidy, "I will very gladly take my leave of the world order."[522] That he lacked air to breathe in his marriage was perhaps expressed in his growing breathing problems, that manifested themselves in tightness in the chest and asthmatic coughing spells. At the same time he was

---

[522] *Ibid.*, March 8, 1881.

plagued by constant digestive disorders and stomach pains, and haunted regularly as well by the disfiguring erysipelas. In the doctors who prescribed copious amounts of medicaments, he had little faith — with justification, as time proved. He suffered (as we know today) from *angina pectoris*, and could have lived longer had he not been treated incorrectly.

As he had to Cosima's attempts at re-education, he reacted to the doctors also with gallows humor. "I see the boxes well," he said referring to the pills and powders on his nightstand, "only I lack the faith."[523] That is how Glasenapp recorded it, who, unlike Cosima, recognized the familiar *Faust* passage. She, by contrast, noted, "'I see the boxes well, however I lack the faith,' he says."[524] He teased his Italian physician, Dr. Cervello, with the sentence, "Doctors always counsel caution because they know well that were one to fall ill, they couldn't help [anyway]!"[525]

When Wagner complained to a certain Professor Schrön in Naples of constant fatigue, he was assured, "It had to be so; he would however return as though rejuvenated, and only at home again would he feel the beneficial effects of his stay here. At this, the Master laughed and said: then I would rather go home at once and benefit from the promised relief."[526] He protested against a stomach probe as an, "Invasion of his personal

---

[523] Glasenapp, v., VI, p. 303. A parody of the declaration Goethe put in the mouth of Faust, "*Die Botschaft hör ich wohl, allein fehlt mir der Glaube.*"
[524] Cosima Wagner, *Diaries*, January 28, 1880. Cosima wrote, "... *doch mir fehlt der Glaube,*" subtly different from Goethe's "... *allein mir fehlt der Glaube,*" but different enough to suggest she did not recognize the quotation.
[525] *Ibid.*, March 12, 1882.
[526] Glasenapp, v. VI, p. 527.

rights!"[527] On the leeches with which Barber Schnappauf regularly bled him, he bestowed the name "the three graces,"[528] and the popular salts for the treatment of flatulence he referred to as "Bullrich von Hutten."[529]

Despite these efforts to make his plight more bearable by tacking on a bit of satire, he fell often into day-long depressions. Quite apart from his health problems, he was trapped in a marital dilemma from which there was no exit: the woman with whom he lived did not want to be the wife he desired, and the woman willing to be that wife did not want to live with him: Judith had no intention whatsoever of renouncing her bohemian life for his sake only to waste away in a provincial German town.

Following the festivals, when Wagner had to bid his beloved farewell, his weariness with life grew more pronounced, and he assured Cosima repeatedly that "he longed for death." With variations, this motif runs like a scarlet thread through the diaries, until the event so often invoked actually occurred. Even its suddenness, Wagner had prophesied trenchantly: "'You shall see,' he once announced to his spouse, 'I will die right under your hand.' Frau Wagner," commented Glasenapp, "rejected this joke with a very stern look, and yet he often repeated it."[530]

Thoughts of death had positively taken possession of his mind. On a trip together in a gondola, which had

---

[527] Cosima Wagner, *Diaries*, January 19, 1883.
[528] Glasenapp, v. VI, p. 527.
[529] Cosima Wagner, *Diaries*, February 6, 1883. "Bullrich Salt" was the name of the remedy; Ullrich von Hutten was an early 16th c. German scholar, poet, and outspoken critic of the Roman Catholic Church.
[530] Glasenapp, v. VI, p. 152.

once before reminded him of death, he said to Cosima, "to endure life, one has to be dead to it."[531] He brooded even over the details, such that his self-irony passed over into the macabre. On one occasion: "he makes a joke about his burial, how I should dress him and accompany him with military salutes, etc.;"[532] on another he reminded Cosima of her former promise, to die together with him: "How shall we make our coffin, what would you prefer, tin or wood?"[533] Ultimately, it was fashioned of bronze with lion's feet, and Cosima hung its key about her neck.

In early February, 1883, after Wagner had taken up residence with his family and staff in a Venetian palazzo following the successful *Parsifal* Festival, there came a furious confrontation with Cosima. The provocation was a young "flower" by the name of Carrie Pringle, who had been among the seductive little flower-maidens in Klingsor's magic garden in the Festival summer of 1882, and afterwards had won Wagner's favor. Her announcement that she would look up the beloved Master at his palazzo came as a surprise.

Cosima blew a fuse. Between her and Wagner, according to their daughter Isolde, there was a "very violent scene," in the course of which Cosima in no uncertain terms prohibited him from receiving the "flower." As his wife played an appropriate piece from her father's repertoire—"In Praise of Tears," by Schubert—her son Siegfried noted on her "an altogether rapt look." On the floor above, her husband died of a heart attack. That was all.

---

[531] *Ibid.*, v. VI, p. 694.
[532] Cosima Wagner, *Diaries*, December 8, 1879.
[533] *Ibid.*, September 27, 1881.

From the viewpoint of his heirs, only a power shift in the dynasty had occurred, which Siegfried Wagner described in 1923 in the sober words: "The 13th of February, 1883, brought a great turn in our lives, above all outwardly. My father had—to use the popular expression—lived from hand to mouth." For the son and heir this had led to the unfortunate consequence that "there were no invested assets." That would soon change. "In the following years, the project became gradually to accumulate wealth."[534] The weighty assignment fell, as would become apparent, under Cosima's jurisdiction.

Two weeks before his death, Wagner had hinted to his wife what he thought of her penchant for forced accumulation of wealth, when he called her "Phylax," after a popular work of the poet and fabulist Christian Fürchtegott Gellert. Wagner had even quoted the first words of the fable in question: "Phylax, who many a night faithfully guarded house and home." To Cosima's query as to the relevance of the poem, he related to her "what an indescribable impression the line 'Phylax came to die!' had left on his childhood." Enthusiastically, she commented, "How gladly, then, I take the name!"[535]

Flattered but unaware, the Cosima had fallen prey to one of Wagner's mystifications. Her husband could allow himself this jest only because he knew she had no idea of the cited poem. Looking back at Gellert's text, it is apparent that the comparison to "Phylax" was absolutely no compliment to her. On the contrary, though the dog in the fable does guard house and home, he is in the process so stingy that even facing

---

[534] Siegfried Wagner, *Erinnerungen*, (Stuttgart, 1923), p. 43.
[535] Cosima Wagner, *Diaries*, January 31, 1883.

imminent death he cannot bring himself to reveal to a fellow creature where he has hidden his "lovely hambone." Gellert's moral, for which Phylax is exemplary:

> "In death, the miser still is stingy.
> He casts two glances on his coffin,
> But a thousand more in terror
> On the hoard he guards in fear.
> O heavy burden of vanity!
> To live badly and die in pain,
> One seeks to pile up goods;
> Does luck like that merit envy?"

It was just as well Cosima did not look up Gellert, if for no other reason than that she could not imagine the Master could be mocking her. The mask he donned for her, she took as the truth. The quote from *Faust* with which her husband on another occasion spoke the truth about their life together, she took as just a joke: "You wander in all deliberate speed with me from heaven through the world to hell."[536]

As an actor at the end of the play removes his mask, the asset-less Wagner took off his velvet beret to die. As he sank onto the small sofa upholstered in pink silk, the gold pocket-watch Cosima had given him fell to the floor. "My watch," were his last words, as though yet conscious of this final irony.[537] What followed, too, must be viewed through the glass of irony: like Saint Catherine, Cosima cut off her hair, and covered her shorn head with Wagner's velvet beret. Five days later, she buried him, just behind Wahnfried, where his dogs already lay in their graves.

---

[536] *Ibid.*, November 21, 1880.
[537] Glasenapp, v. VI, p. 774.

The Laughing Wagner

"The Witty Person is Missing." On Wagner's death in 1883, the Viennese *Figaro* opined that *sans* the immortal Master the angels could barely hold back, his work of Bayreuth was left in the cold.

No, his "final triumph" was not granted him, of bringing them "all to laughter in my dying hour."[538] Somehow, death in Venice, as befell him there on the Grand Canal, did not suit him—though it suited Cosima very well, who taking the part of the grand tragedienne played funereal music by Liszt, then,

---

[538] Cosima Wagner, *Diaries*, May 19, 1880.

according to her small son Siegfried, gave voice to the "force of the most passionate pain," before slipping into the role of the Great Mourner, which she did not relinquish to the day of her death 47 years later.

Of the laughing Wagner, there seemed nothing left. Cosima banished him from her cult, despite knowing better. For even in the final months of his life, he had concerned himself with the comic — not in the familiar form of bourgeois comedy, but in its primal manifestation in folk and puppet-theater. As he had begun his artistic career with his own hand-sewn marionettes, he ended it now in reminiscence of those early beginnings, revived by readings of the old *Faust* puppet-plays, and visits to the Venetian folk theater.

Already in the pre-Bayreuth time, he had admitted that for him, the "authentic German theatrical folk-spirit" was to be found not in Nordic mythology, but most originally in the "Kasperl-theater of our annual fairs." Its players embodied for him the true "spirit of the theater," for here, according to Wagner, "the improviser was poet, director, and actor at once, and through his magic his poor puppets came to life for me with the truthfulness of the imperishable folk characters." In short, "in that Kasperl-theater, I saw the birthplace of German drama before me."[539]

Time and again he studied the old "Puppet Comedy of Faust,"[540] and in the Tribschen period even planned his own version: "Richard speaks often of a 'Kasperl' he would like to write and compose. Kasperl and Wagner are the main characters, Faust in the background,"[541]

---

[539] Wagner, *Sämtliche Schriften und Dichtungen*, v. IX, p. 181.
[540] Cosima Wagner, *Diaries*, October 2, 1870.
[541] *Ibid.*, February 23, 1869.

Cosima recorded. On another occasion, he identified himself with the clown, of whom he said, "this is the human being as animal,"[542] or with the disrespectful Kasperl, who gives everyone a knock. After reading Cosima a newly drafted letter, he summed up its contents in the tone of Kasperl: "So, now I've knocked his block off."[543] Just weeks before his death, when the traditional comic intrigue *Le baruffe Chiozzotte* ("Much Noise in Chiozza") by Goldoni—over which Wagner had enthused already in the *Tristan* period in Venice— was given, he was determined to see it again. We returned "home entirely satisfied," Cosima wrote. "Play and performance alike delighted us."[544]

Central to his Venetian hankering for the traditional theater, which contrasted so markedly with Cosima's Bayreuth art-cult, stood the figure of Harlequin, the clever and shameless joker with half-mask and patchwork costume. Since this enigmatic character, whose name derives from the Italian word for "little devil," stands above things, he can, as a witty improviser, freely say aloud everything others dare not. No wonder the theater of the Enlightenment took exception to Harlequin's fool's liberty, did away with him summarily, and burned him on the public stage.

This symbolic *auto-da-fé* did actually take place. The spectacular immolation of Harlequin was mounted in 1737 by the puritanical theater-reformer Karoline Neuber in Leipzig, who simultaneously drove out the clown and the improvisatory art of the *Commedia dell'arte* from the German stage. The time of improvisation had run out, and art advanced to the

---

[542] *Ibid.*, October 5, 1871.
[543] *Ibid.*, June 28, 1880.
[544] *Ibid.*, January 1, 1883.

humorless quasi-religion, the "moral educational institution."

Before his death in Venice, Wagner often sang a Harlequin's song, which contrasted strangely with the solemn tones of his *Parsifal*. He himself identified the song-repertoire of his first wife, Minna, as the origin of the song, although it might just as well be associated with Carlo Collodis's children's book *Pinocchio*, in which a wooden Harlequin faces the prospect of a fiery death.

"Harlequin must die," the song was called, and when Wagner played it for his guests on his Ibach piano, he sang the refrain, "Harlequin, you must diiiiiiiiiiiiiieeeeeeeee,"[545] in a tone of comic despair. On another occasion, he improvised appropriate funeral music, characterized by Cosima as a "grandiose funereal *intrada*, proceeded by 'Harlequin, you must die,' then in turn reversion to the solemn music."[546] Occasionally, "he plays the very elaborate Harlequin improvisation with '*Du lieber Augustin!*' at the end," which Wagner elucidated with the words: "Death now dances with Harlequin."[547]

He himself danced once more. One month before his death, Cosima recorded how while her father played Beethoven, jester-like, he "twice entered the room dancing."[548] His son Siegfried also recalled: "Suddenly, at the scherzo, we see our father enter and dance, unremarked by Liszt or the [other] listeners, in

---

[545] *Ibid.*, January 31, 1883. "*Harlekin, du mußt sterererrrrerrrebenenene.*"
[546] *Ibid.*, January 15, 1883.
[547] *Ibid.*, January 16, 1883.
[548] *Ibid.*, January 10, 1883.

the most skillful and graceful way. One could have thought one saw before one a youth of twenty years."

A final image of Harlequin: for the finale of Carnival on February 6, 1883, Wagner will not forgo attending the closing show of the feast of fools with his family. St. Mark's Square, filled with colorful costumes and masks, is brightly lit with gas candelabras; masked couples flock onto the dance floor, which is encircled with flickering coal braziers. Emerging from the narrow passages, from the bridges and quais ever new masked and costumed revelers press into the square, step out of torch-bearing gondolas, others yelling, toss bouquets and flowers from the windows, while the sounds of trumpets and singing drift through from all directions.

On the ringing of a bell from the clock-tower, everyone looks towards the *Santa Maria della Salute*, where on the Grand Canal a grand festival flotilla approaches. Torch light across the black water heralds the first boats, which, filled with masked revelers and musicians, group themselves about a large gondola under whose canopy the Prince of the Carnival and his Princess sit enthroned as larger-than-life, fantastically outfitted puppets.

As cannons are fired and rockets whiz into the night sky, then explode into a colorful shimmering shower of sparks, the gondola lands at the columns with the St. Mark lions and Saint Theodor at the water's edge. Between them, pressed about on all sides by the waiting throng, rises a forbidding pyre, around which the executioner's workmen pile the last bundles of straw.

For the Prince of the Carnival and his beloved must die. No sooner has the funeral train with the giant puppets reached the place of the *auto-da-fé*, than their decorated Highnesses are lifted onto the pile, and bound to stakes. To the wild cries of the revelers, a torch flies in a high arc into the straw, flames lick the air, and the baroque costumes go up in crackling flames. As the couple blazes up and the pale smoke rises, thudding cannon-fire echoes across the lagoon, answered by the celebratory cries of the crowd.

As the blazing, building-high fire collapses into itself, the last reflections flash in the windows of the Doge's Palace. Motionless, the people stand around the pile, from which only small flames still dart, and begin to remove their masks. The music has stilled, the Prince and his beloved have been burnt to a small pile of ashes. "But the midnight bell and the dying of the flames have a lovely effect," Cosima noted. When the gas candelabras have also been extinguished, the people leave the square, over which hang clouds of smoke.

Richard Wagner has seen enough. The gondola which days later will carry his bronze casket to the railway station, returns him now to the *Palazzo Vendramin*. To the doorman, who helps him out of the gondola, he says, "*Amico mio, il Carnevale e andato!*"[549]

"My friend, the Carnival is over!"

---

[549] Otto, p. 623.

Epilogue

On May 12, 1872, as his impresario Angelo Neumann[550] recounted, Wagner conducted a Beethoven concert at the New Vienna *Musikverein* Hall. During the performance, the horn virtuoso Richard Lewy had the misfortune "to crack a note, or as one says, to squeak."[551] The comic dramatist Eduard Mautner, who was sitting in the front row, and as critic of the *New Free Press* was thoroughly familiar with Wagner's theses about "Judaism in Music," laughed maliciously.

During the intermission, Wagner was seen hurrying over to Mautner. Instead of thanking him for ridiculing the horn player, however, the Master, outraged, explained to him that "it is a violation to mock a wind player on account of a cracked note. One must understand what it means to coax the perfect sound from the brittle metal, and how the greatest artistry can come a cropper on a tiny drop of saliva." Demonstratively, the Bayreuth Master embraced the Jewish artist, who had followed his elucidations in amazement.

But for Richard Lewy, the matter was not therewith concluded. "Dear Mautner," he said to the comic writer, "it was unkind of you to laugh at my cracked note — and ungrateful, too."

---

[550] Neumann, p. 8.
[551] Among American brass players, colloquially, the corresponding term is to play a "clam," or "to clam."

Mautner eyed him quizzically.

"For you see," Lewy explained, "I have been to every one of your comedies, and haven't laughed a single time."

The Laughing Wagner

Joachim Köhler

INDEX of NAMES

Adam, Theodor	151
Addison, Joseph	58, 130
Adorno, Theodor W.	24
Aeschylus	173, 174
Apel, Theodor	67-8
Bakunin, Michail	81, 138, 146
Beethoven, Ludwig van	48, 53, 61-8, 88, 109, 144, 195, 246, 249
Bell, Alexander	14
Berlioz, Hector	109, 117, 146
Brandt, Marianne	197 ff.
Bruckner, Anton	34
Bülow, Cosima von	17
Bülow, Hans von	91, 154, 157, 207, 224
Callot, Jacques	39, 93, 101, 42n.
Chorley, Henry F.	123 ff., 129
Collodi, Carlo	246
Cornelius, Peter	17, 141, 220
d'Agoult, Marie	220, 223-24
Davison, James	132
Dessauer, Josef	98 ff.
Devrient, Eduard	8
Doepler, Carl Emil	56
Döll, Heinrich	196
Dorn, Heinrich	62 ff., 117, 119
Eckstein, Friedrich	209-10
Edison, Thomas	193

Fontane, Theodor	173
Fourcaud, Louis de	4
Friedrich August (King of Saxony)	19
Friedrich Wilhelm IV.	144
Gaillard, Karl	89
Gaul, Franz	122
Gautier, Judith	182, 205-10, 215, 230, 239
Gellert, Christian Fürchtegott	241-42
Geyer, Ludwig,	6, 19-21, 47
Glasenapp, Carl Friedrich	4, 64, 79, 85, 178, 190, 195, 204, 208, 210, 217, 238, 239
Goethe, Johann Wolfgang von	13 n., 60, 144, 195, 233, 236, 238 n.
Gregor-Dellin, Martin	24, 26, 103
Grimm (Brothers)	183
Gutmann, Robert	26
Gutzkow, Karl	115, 118, 139-41
Hanslick, Eduard	89, 163-68, 184, 192, 194
Haydn, Joseph	62
Heckel, Emil	150
Heckel, Karl	221
Hecker, Friedrich	190
Heine, Ferdinand	86, 139, 222
Heine, Heinrich	5, 66, 96, 101, 104, 120, 129, 142, 190 n.
Heine, Marie	86
Herwegh, Emma	26, 76
Heyse, Paul	115
Hiller, Ferdinand	144
Hoffrnann, E.T.A.	36, 39-48, 52-3, 64-6, 76, 85, 92, 98-103, 140, 169, 171
Hugo, Victor	161
Humperdinck, Engelbert	191, 195-96
Hünerfürst, Hugo	142

Jank, Christian	196
Janz, Curt Paul	214
Keller, Gottfried	115, 227-29
Kienlen, Johann Christoph	60, 66
Kienzl, Wilhelm	219
Kietz, Ernst Benedikt	101-04, 133, 194
Kietz, Gustav Adolph	10, 87
Konstantin (Prince of Saxony)	19, 20, 54, 76
Lablache, Luigi	170-71
Lassalle, Ferdinand	226
Laube, Heinrich	121, 137-38, 163
Laussot, Jessie	78, 207
Lehmann, Lilli	54, 225
Lehrs, Samuel	105
Lenbach, Franz von	215
Lesimple, August	160
Levi, Hermann	226-27
Lewy, Richard	249-50
Lindau, Paul	146 n., 182
Liszt, Franz	33, 145-46, 162, 182, 186, 190, 199, 207, 210, 213, 219, 223-24, 235, 243, 246
Ludwig II (King of Bavaria)	14, 107, 155-59, 168, 196
Mann, Thomas	4, 33, 101, 113
Marie Antoinette	83
Materna, Amelie	196-98
Mautner Eduard	249-50
Mendelssohn Bartholdy, Felix	117-24, 139, 144-46, 166
Meser, Carl Friedrich	152-53
Meyerbeer, Giacomo	96-7, 101, 117-28, 139-40
Meysenbug, Malwida von	45, 109, 214
Mottl, Felix	188, 194
Mozart, Wolfgang Amedeus	60, 66

Muchanow, Marie	190
Napoleon Bonaparte	25-6
Nestroy, Johann	74, 141-43, 155, 161, 166, 187
Neuber, Karoline	245
Neumann, Angelo	35 n., 147, 181, 185, 249
Nietzsche, Friedrich	2, 3, 6, 18, 133, 140 n., 154, 158, 162, 164, 174, 192, 211-20, 225
Nohl, Ludwig	168
Offenbach, Jacques	161, 163
Ollivier, Emile	7
Otto, August	14
Pecht, Friedrich	25, 144, 222
Petipa, Lucien	29, 136
Philippi, Felix	198
Planer, Minna, see Wagner, Minna	
Pohl, Richard	91
Praeger, Ferdinand	37, 84, 91
Pringle, Carrie	240
Rhyn, Angelique am	44
Richter, Hans	161, 166
Ritter, Karl	39
Röckel, August	139
Rolland, Romain	226
Ross, Werner	214
Rossini, Giacomo	159, 170, 180
Rubinstein, Joseph	158, 162, 196
Schemann, Ludwig	126
Schladebach, Julius	119-20
Schnappauf,, Bernhard (barber)	111, 208, 215, 239
Schnorr von Carolsfeld, Ludwig (tenor)	31
Schnorr von Carolsfeld, Veit (painter)	144

Schopenhauer, Arthur	176
Schröder-Devrient, Wilhelmine	67, 134-35, 138, 207
Schumann, Clara	61
Schumann, Robert	96, 116, 124, 132, 144
Schuré, Edouard	8
Shakespeare, William	33, 47-8, 53
Sontag, Henriette	144-46
Sophocles	59
Speidel, Ludwig	184
Strauss, Franz	198
Strauss, Richard	198
Thode, Henry	159
Tichatschek, Joseph	135, 142
Tieck, Ludwig	144
Träger, Adolf	25
Tchaikovsky, Peter	117
Turgenev, Ivan	123
Viardot-Garcia, Pauline	95
Victoria (Queen)	90-91
Voltaire	212-15
Wagner, Adolf	40, 48, 50, 59
Wagner, Albert	213-14
Wagner, Cäcilie	20, 37
Wagner, Clara	20-21, 60
Wagner, Cosima	2-3, 8, 17, 21, 23, 33, 38, 44-45, 49, 54, 80, 85, 88, 107-11, 125-26, 131, 151, 155, 157-62, 176, 182-248
Wagner, Eva	89
Wagner, Friedrich	20, 40
Wagner, Isolde	155, 240
Wagner, Julius	126-27
Wagner, Luise	20
Wagner, Minna	72-91, 94, 100-06, 137, 148, 156, 246

Wagner, Nathalie	79, 81
Wagner, Ottilie	20, 50
Wagner, Rosalie	20
Wagner, Rosine	20-21
Wagner, Siegfried	155, 241, 244, 246
Wallnöfer, Adolf	185
Walter, Bruno	154
Weber, Carl Maria von	19, 22, 46-7, 60-1, 129, 144
Weihermüller, Konrad	189
Weingartner, Felix	174
Weinlig, Theodor	62
Weißheimer, Wendelin	30, 158, 168, 185
Wesendonck, Mathilde von	9, 92, 156, 186, 207
Wesendonck, Otto von	156, 165 n.
Wieck, Friedrich	61
Wilhelm I. (German Kaiser)	13, 15, 54
Willich, Cäsar	9-10
Winter, Ludwig	151
Wolzogen, Hans von	38, 162

ABOUT THE AUTHOR

Joachim Köhler, born in 1952, is a German cultural historian specializing in 19th century philosophy and art. The subject of his 1977 doctoral dissertation was Friedrich Nietzsche, who has remained the central focus of his research. Also a topic of major scholarly interest has been the life and work of Richard Wagner. Köhler's three major books on Nietzsche and Wagner, translated into many languages, are published in the U.S. by Yale University Press. *The Laughing Wagner* is his first book with *Free Scholar Press*.

THE TRANSLATOR

Tom Artin is the author most recently of *The Wagner Complex*. He has translated numerous books, primarily from German, and he serves as editor and publisher of *Free Scholar Press*.

Printed in Great Britain
by Amazon